MW01199451

Understanding the Value of ISO 9000

A Management Guide
to
Higher Quality, Productivity, and Sales

SPC Press, Inc.
Knoxville, Tennessee

Understanding the Value of ISO 9000

A Management Guide
to
Higher Quality, Productivity, and Sales

Dr. Bryn Owen, Quality Consultant
Optimum Systems for Quality, Ltd..

Peter Malkovich, Quality Consultant
East Concord Associates

Catherine Malkovich, Editor

SPC Press, Inc.
Knoxville, Tennessee

Copyright © 1995 Process Management International, Inc.

ALL RIGHTS RESERVED
No portion of this work may be reproduced by any means whatsoever
without the prior written permission of the publisher:

SPC Press, Inc.
5908 Toole Drive, Suite C
Knoxville, Tennessee 37919   U.S.A.
(615) 584-5005

Several quotations from the ISO 9001 Standard are found in the book.
They are taken from ANSI/ASQC Q9001-1994,
published in the U.S. by ASQC.
These quotations are used with the permission of ASQC.

For information about:
Achieving ISO 9000 Registration:
A Process Management Approach
to the Optimum Quality System
by Owen, Malkovich, Cothran

or

Understanding the Value of ISO 9000
A Management Guide to Higher Quality, Productivity, and Sales
by Owen and Malkovich

or

For a free catalog of books published by SPC Press,
Call 1-800-545-8602

SPC Graphics Editor:
Chris McAlister

SPC Press Technical Editor:
David Wheeler

ISBN 0-945320-44-2

1 2 3 4 5 6 7 8 9

Table of Contents

Foreword

All managers operate under pressure. At any time, however, in addition to problems to be solved that day or faced next week, there are those issues which would be good to do "when the recent reorganization has bedded down" or "when we have time." One issue that can fall into this black hole is accredited certification of the company's quality management system—unless, that is, purchasers are saying, "Achieve it if you want to do business with us."

This book, however, not only makes the overwhelming case for giving accredited certification of the company's quality management system a higher priority but encourages the manager to see how it can be achieved. It faces up to the effort required and does not pretend that the process is a quick fix. What it does do, however, is take the progressive, but initially perhaps doubting, manager through the stages involved. It explains the steps, it provides the options, it illustrates from the experience of others. By this means it seeks to give confidence to the individual competent manager that, using his range of management skills, this is something that he and his colleagues can achieve for their company. Its aim is to convince them that the process is more than worth the effort, which if sustained will continue to pay dividends in terms of efficiency, market share, and profitability over years to come.

Whether the book succeeds in this will be for the practitioners to judge, but no one who has read this book should be surprised at what the process of achieving accredited certification involves, nor hopefully disappointed in the benefits which accrue.

J. D. G. Hammer, CB,
Chairman
National Accreditation Council for Certification Bodies

Acknowledgments

The authors are first indebted to their clients and colleagues who have enriched their consulting practices and taught them so much.

We thank Stewart Judd, Joel Finley, Roger King, Jack Whitaker, Ed Payne, Andrew Libberton, Knute Gilbertson, and Mike Keefe, who reviewed the early manuscript and provided insight and input. Scott Jensen did his usual superb job of crafting the figures.

We also thank Jim Hammer for reviewing the book and writing the Foreword.

About the Authors

The authors, Bryn Owen and Peter M. Malkovich, share a wide range of experience and specialized knowledge that makes them ideally suited to write this book. Their international work in management, engineering, and the quality movement—work spread across many different industries—provides a strong cognitive and experiential foundation for this book. Dr. Owen and Mr. Malkovich are also two of the authors of *Achieving ISO 9000 Registration: A Process Management Approach to the Optimum Quality System*, a widely-acclaimed book which provides cogent directions for any business that is seeking registration to the Standard.

Dr. Bryn Owen developed the Process Management Model for the implementation of ISO 9000. A founder of Optimum Systems for Quality, Ltd., since 1987 he has worked with over 100 clients who have successfully used this model to develop systems that meet the requirements of the Standard, while at the same time, improving their internal operations. Clients have included a wide range of service and manufacturing industries and government departments.

Dr. Owen has trained as a Quality Systems Lead Auditor. His undergraduate degrees are in Industrial Engineering and Management Studies. He also has an MSc for studies related to Metrology and Quality Control. His doctoral work (studies in the implementation of ISO 9000 in manufacturing industries) was completed in 1991 at Salford University College.

At Salford University College, he served as the Principal Lecturer in Engineering, specifically responsible for courses in quality and computer-aided engineering. He has held positions in management and quality systems both in England and Nigeria.

Peter M. Malkovich is the President and founder of East Concord Associates. He has assisted many organizations, including his former employer, in achieving ISO 9000 registration.

Mr. Malkovich has over 30 years of business, industrial, and consulting experience. He has worked as an engineer, in engineering management, and has held senior staff and line management positions in both manufacturing and service organizations.

He holds a Bachelor of Mechanical Engineering degree (with honors) and an MBA. While working on a Ph.D. at the University of Minnesota, he taught courses in the School of Business.

His consulting assignments have been numerous and diverse including technical projects, strategic planning, total quality, reengineering, and business acquisitions/divestitures. Consulting assignments have taken him to Japan, Israel, Austria, the Netherlands, and the United Kingdom.

Overview of Book

This book is written for the decision-makers and influencers in all kinds of organizations—both those that provide products and service organizations. In this book we primarily address the issue of *how to benefit from registration to the Standard,* rather than how to achieve registration. Essentially, this book begins at management's decision point—and carries the reader far beyond the ending point of most ISO 9000 books.

Our earlier book, *Achieving ISO 9000 Registration: A Process Management Approach to the Optimum Quality System*, presents the Process Management Approach to efficiently and effectively register an organization to an ISO 9000 standard. Essentially, it is a "how-to" book for the implementation team.

ISO 9000 is for all organizations—industrial and commercial, manufacturing and service, public and private, large and small. Our clients have ranged in size from as few as two to several thousand employees. Our experience is as diverse as it is extensive. We have worked with government agencies as well as organizations that manufacture products and process materials. Other clients have been organizations that provide recreation, nursing, banking, engineering, and consulting services. The book distills our experience in assisting over 150 organizations achieve registration.

This book is structured as diagrammed on page *xv*. It examines the issues associated with achieving ISO 9000 registration, especially with realizing an acceptable return on the investment.

Chapter 1 relates ISO 9000 to the operation of an organization and explains why ISO 9000 is management's responsibility.

Chapter 2 addresses the ISO 9000 decision factors—what is involved in getting registered, what it may cost, how long it will take, and the benefits to be gained—information needed to make the initial ISO 9000 decision.

Chapter 3 covers the benefits attainable from ISO 9000—benefits that make ISO 9000 registration a winning investment. If registration is approached with high expectations, and if an efficient and effective quality system is implemented, the organization will realize huge benefits. This chapter discusses the typical benefits as well as potential benefits that are missed by many registered organizations. To maximize benefits, the implementation process must be proper and thorough, and a value-adding quality system must be installed. The rest of the chapters discuss how these requirements can be managed and ensured.

Chapters 4 and 5 focus on *management—the key to benefiting from registration to ISO 9000*. Key decisions and choices and management's role are covered. The technical staff can achieve registration, but management must work to ensure benefits.

In Chapter 4, the Process Management Approach to ISO 9000 registration is introduced.

Chapter 5 defines management's leadership and role during the registration process as well as after registration is achieved.

Chapter 6 discusses the key steps in the registration process.

Chapter 7 is a reference guide to keep the registration process on course over the long implementation period.

The appendices include useful reference material:

    A. ISO 9000 Compliance Check – A self-assessment tool to estimate level of compliance with the Standard's requirements.

    B. A Detailed Review – ISO 9001 – A detailed review of the requirements of ISO 9001.

C. Implementation Plan Guidelines – Plans for achieving registration in 8, 12, and 18 months.
D. Lists of Procedures – Typical lists of procedures for a manufacturing company and a service company.
E. Sample Procedure – A sample procedure illustrating the format and content.
F. Changes in the ISO 9000 Standards – The evolution of the ISO 9000 Standard.
G. Where to Go for Help – Sources for consulting and training assistance.

Let's start off by being straightforward—organizations that want to get registered to ISO 9000 can do it. World-wide, nearly 100,000 organizations are registered. It's not that difficult. The real challenge, and more critical issue, is to gain more than a registration certificate from your ISO 9000 effort and investment. This is management's job. Management needs to ensure that the outcome of its investment includes:

- a better-running business,
- happier customers,
- higher sales, and
- a system that provides ongoing, continuous improvement of the entire organization.

The achievement of these outcomes is management's responsibility. The objective of this book is to show management that these outcomes are achievable and the natural result of a structured approach to registration.

ISO 9000

Chapter 1: ISO 9000 – The Standard for Management

- Why ISO 9000 is for management
- ISO 9000 means more than the registration certificate
- An opportunity for long-term impact

Chapter 2: ISO 9000 – Your Decision

- What ISO 9000 is
- Why get registered
- What's involved in registration
- What it costs and how long it takes
- The ISO 9000 decision

Benefits Beyond the Certificate

Chapter 3: The ISO 9000 Pay-back

- Benefits from implementation
  - Improved processes
  - Reengineering
- Benefits from registration
  - Market advantage
  - Continual improvement
  - Fewer "fires"
  - Quality culture
- Benefits beyond registration
  - Total company
  - Total Quality Management (TQM)
  - Process management

If It's Done Right!

Chapter 4: Key Decisions

- Scope of registration
- The optimum quality system
- Setting objectives
- Using outside assistance
- Internal resources and organization
- Effective internal audits
- Selecting a registrar
- Pre-assessment audit

Chapter 5: Management's Role

- Leading the project to get registered
- Developing a quality policy
- Communicating to the organization
- Chairing management reviews
- Internal auditing
- Impacting the functional areas

Chapter 6: What Needs to Be Done

- The nine steps to registration
  - Prepare for the project
  - Analyze and evaluate existing processes
  - Optimize processes
  - Document and approve the quality system
  - Train internal auditors and prepare to operate the system
  - Operate and refine the documented system
  - Verify readiness
  - Prepare for the registration audit
  - Registration audit and registration
- After registration
  - Surveillance audits
  - Operating the system

Book Organization Diagram

It seems that most executives view ISO 9000 as a quality certification program that recognizes the organization for satisfying an ISO 9000 quality standard. The tendency is for management to designate an implementation team to get the organization registered and become involved, as needed, throughout the project. The ISO 9000 certificate showing compliance and registration is the objective or "end."

We don't view ISO 9000 this way and we don't think you should either. ISO 9000 needs to be viewed as a "means," not an "end"—a means to a more controlled, consistent, and effective operation; to more satisfied customers, and a more competitive and successful business. That's what this book is all about.

Chapter One

ISO 9000
The Standard for Management

In This Chapter:

- Why ISO 9000 is for management
- There is more to ISO 9000 than the registration certificate
- Opportunities for positive impact on performance and competitiveness

The main premise of this book is that there is more to ISO 9000 registration than a certificate for the wall. Realizing the extra benefits and achieving acceptable returns from the ISO 9000 investment are management's duty. The benefits, costs, and hence, the returns from ISO 9000 are determined by management's role and the decisions it makes while pursuing and maintaining registration. This chapter explains why ISO 9000 is for management. The remainder of the book discusses management's role and the important decisions managers must make.

ISO 9000 Is for Management

ISO 9000 is about managing the business—managing it in such a way that it is continually improving and becoming more competitive. The ISO 9000 Standards define the requirements for a

1

quality system. The requirements are good, common-sense business practices that could just as well have been called *Management System Requirements*. Fortunately, they weren't. Announcing that "we are going to improve the management system" is not likely to inspire employees. But ask them to help improve the quality system, and you get a different response. Everyone wants to improve quality.

Most managers think they are doing a good job. If you tell them you want to evaluate and improve the management system, they take it personally. But tell managers that this is a program to improve the quality system, and just like other employees, they respond positively. Let's be pleased that ISO 9000 is about quality systems!

We think you will agree that good business practice includes:

- employees who know what needs to be done,
- clear policies that are understood by all,
- processes capable of meeting requirements,
- clear and honest communication with customers,
- suppliers that understand and meet requirements,
- use of customer and process information,
- a staff trained and developed to meet the needs of the business, and
- appropriate responses to performance data.

Such practices are necessary if an organization is to successfully identify, define, and meet the needs and expectations of customers. They are also the major operational requirements of the ISO 9000 Standards. ISO 9000 is good business practice and all about operating the business—*clearly management's responsibility.*

It is not sufficient just to operate the business. All businesses, and indeed all organizations, need to have a purpose for their existence—*clearly management's responsibility.*

"Purpose" is defined in terms of goals, objectives, vision, and mission. A clear definition of purpose is a prerequisite for success. Indeed, without it, success cannot be measured. In today's competitive environment, the purpose has to be customer-focused and still address the needs and expectations of employees and owners.

ISO 9000 requires a quality policy; that is, a statement which sets forth the aims and expectations of the organization regarding quality and satisfying customers. This policy must be customer-focused and must be aligned with the organization's purpose.

To achieve that purpose, defined strategies and plans are required, and their implementation requires feedback and control. Systems provide control. The more complex the business, the more complex the system. Without a viable system, the business is like a rudderless ship out on the ocean.

A quality or management system is a control system, and the ISO 9000 Standards detail the requirements. The system ensures that what needs to happen does, in fact, happen. It ensures a particular level of quality—quality products, quality service, quality staff, quality communication, and quality management. It is a means of controlling the processes and a means for the organization to meet its objectives and achieve its purpose.

The quality system supports the business, but the employees operate the system to enable the organization to meet its objectives. The system defines their roles and responsibilities, describes the work they do, and determines how they interrelate.

Understanding the relationships between individuals is a key to understanding the quality system. Individuals work together but have separate roles. They are all customers and suppliers of each other. The quality of service they provide each other is critical if the business is to meet its objectives. All employees must address and meet the needs and expectations of their internal customers rather than compete against each other in a structural hierarchy.

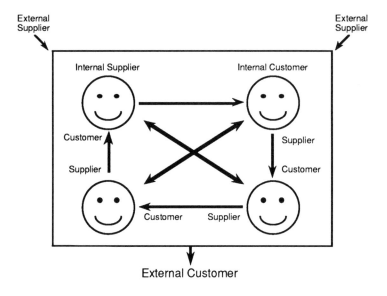

Figure 1.1   People in Systems

The quality system describes the communication within the business—the information flow throughout the system. The efficiency of communication clearly affects the efficiency of the business. The receivers of information are the customers of the senders; their needs and expectations must be considered. Because much of the communication goes from management to staff, managers are suppliers to their staff. They need to consider the needs of the receivers and ensure that all communication is clearly understandable. Management of the quality system is, in part, about efficient communication—*clearly management's responsibility.*

When things go wrong, it is most likely a system problem, not a worker problem. It is a failure on the part of management—*clearly management's responsibility.* Poor materials, inadequate equipment, low levels of maintenance, and misleading instructions all cause problems with quality and are the direct responsibility of management. Problems with motivation and training are management responsibilities as well.

After a major product recall, we heard one chief executive state, "I am not responsible for what went wrong, but I am going to make sure it never happens again." If, after the fact, he can "make sure it never happens again," he should have been able to prevent it from happening in the first place. The chief executive is always responsible for the operation of the organization and must ensure that its quality system is efficient and meets the organization's needs.

Obviously the chief executive cannot be expected to validate every decision. Delegation is essential. But for delegation not to become abdication, it must include control. Such control is provided by the quality system.

The ISO 9000 requirements are general and not prescriptive. They describe features and characteristics of a good quality management system. Organizations of all sizes and types are assessed to the same requirements. Management has to decide how best to satisfy the requirements for the business.

A sailboat and a nuclear submarine can both cross the Atlantic, but their commanders will undoubtedly use different routes and definitely require different control systems. Both need to know where they are going, have a means of measuring their current positions, have a trained crew, and keep a log of their progress. These are common to both voyages, but each commander achieves them in a different way, appropriately and, hopefully, in the optimum way to the respective environments.

So it is in business. All quality systems are, and need to be, different. Each business needs an optimal quality system for its purpose—*clearly management's responsibility.* The quality system is the basis upon which the business is run, and it deserves top priority. It is incumbent upon management to develop its quality system.

ISO 9000:
More than a Registration Certificate

Every organization already has a quality system. Each has an infrastructure that enables it to identify, define, and meet customer needs and expectations. This infrastructure is the quality system, and it probably already satisfies many of the Standard's requirements. ISO 9000 requirements are general and not very stringent.

ISO 9000 registration itself may provide market differentiation today, but it won't for long. Your competitors can easily attain registration and most, no doubt, will. If you are looking to the certificate as your only objective, your sights are much too low. If you don't implement an efficient, value-adding quality system, you will not only be neutralized by the competition but ultimately disadvantaged. A poorly designed and implemented quality system quickly turns from an advantage to a disadvantage as competitors become registered.

> *The British predecessor of ISO 9000 started in the early 1980s, and registrations accelerated in the United Kingdom during that decade. Today, over 60 percent of worldwide registered sites are located there. But in 1991, we started getting calls from registered firms in the United Kingdom asking for our help in redesigning their quality systems. These callers realized that their quality systems were more of a hindrance than a help.*

ISO 9000:
An Opportunity for Long-Term Impact

ISO 9000 registration can be the catalyst for change and a provider of benefits for any organization. Remember, ISO 9000 is about operating and managing the business. The process of preparing for registration, using the registration, and going beyond its requirements provides opportunities to change and benefit the organization. Chapter 3 discusses these opportunities in more detail.

Preparing for ISO 9000 Registration

An early step in the registration project is examining the existing operation for compliance to the Standard. Processes should be examined to determine their effectiveness in meeting performance objectives and their alignment with the overall business purpose. This self-analysis provides an opportunity to identify shortcomings and implement improvements.

Once improved and optimized, processes are then documented. Procedures are written to describe processes and define responsibilities and objectives. The documented system is the basis for standardization, consistency in operation, and understanding among employees—resulting in more trouble-free operations.

By registration time, the business has an improved understanding of its processes, has shaped the staff into a team with common objectives, and is more customer-focused—all real benefits of ISO 9000.

Using the Registration

The ISO 9000 registration certificate is required by some customers. Gaining it has an immediate market benefit, although that benefit may be short-lived.

But ISO 9000 requirements provide the mechanism and discipline to continually improve the system and the business. Registering to ISO 9000 does not mean you achieve perfection. Halos and wings are not issued with the certificate. ISO 9000 registration does mean, however, that every time something goes wrong, the problem is viewed as an opportunity to improve. *The emphasis is on prevention rather than cure;* a major mind-set change at all levels.

The emphasis on quality in preparing for registration increases quality awareness throughout the entire work force. Understanding that quality is about satisfying customer needs and expectations makes the entire organization more customer-focused and brings improvements in quality. This translates to customer confidence in, and growth for, the business.

Beyond ISO 9000 Registration

Changes in attitude lead to total quality and continual improvement. ISO 9000 is the foundation, or platform, for a more comprehensive quality and management system. It is the basis for process management. Both are essential to succeed in today's competitive market.

Summary

ISO 9000 is an international standard for quality systems. A quality system is really a management system that defines how the business is run to meet customer needs. ISO 9000 is management's responsibility and it requires management's attention. This book focuses on the management roles and responsibilities to ensure registration is efficiently achieved and that a value-adding quality system results. Only then can the maximum benefits be realized.

ISO 9000 means changes and improvements to the business. The resulting benefits can produce a high return on investment. A committed and involved management team can make it happen.

Have you decided to seek ISO 9000 registration? If so, Chapter Two can help you plan the project. It also provides background information to help you communicate with and provide general training for your organization.

If you haven't yet decided whether to work toward registration, this chapter provides information to help you make the decision—what ISO 9000 is; why companies are becoming registered and how they benefit; what's involved in getting registered; how long it takes; and the cost.

Chapter Two

ISO 9000
Your Decision

In This Chapter:

- What is quality, a quality system, and ISO 9000?
- Why seek registration?
- Benefits of registration
- What is required to achieve registration?
- How long will it take?
- What will it cost?
- The ISO 9000 decision

Quality

What is quality?... A quality system?... ISO 9000? More than 2,000 years ago Plato defined quality using the example of a flute-player and flute-maker. In those days, when a player wanted a new flute, he would find a craftsman and tell him what he had in mind. Together they would test and refine the design until the flute was exactly what the player wanted. The player defined the requirements and the quality.

We have to remember that the days when the player and the maker knew each other were simpler times; today they rarely meet.

Not only will the flute not be made in our town, it probably won't even be made in our country. Its parts might be made in several countries and shipped to still another country for assembly.

There is little opportunity today for an individual such as the flute player to have one-on-one influence on the design and development of a product or service. Instead, the product or service is presented, and we have two choices—to buy or not to buy. If we choose not to buy, there's a good chance the supplier or manufacturer will never know the reason.

But we do have opportunities to voice our displeasure or satisfaction with products and services. By buying a certain product, we influence the market. For example, you plan to buy a pair of jeans. The "brand name" jeans costs twice as much as the others, and yet, both look the same when compared at the store. But what happens after they've been worn and washed? Therein lies the difference! You can throw the high-priced name brand into the washer and drier and they come out looking like new, fitting as they did before. And the others? The legs are now two inches shorter, and if you can get the zipper up and the button closed, you forfeit your ability to breathe. It's no secret which ones you will buy next time.

Many of us speak nostalgically about "the good old days." Some yearn for the small town where they grew up—where everybody knew their name. Increasing numbers of our citizens are acting on their dreams, leaving the cities and suburbs and returning to small towns. They speak of regaining the "quality of life" that had been lost to them. They have found places where the flute-maker and the flute-player still know and respect each other and maybe even turn out a quality product together. But the reality is that for most of us, those days are gone forever.

In the "real" world there are varying levels of quality which can be classified into three zones as shown in Figure 2.1. There is a deficient zone, a neutral zone, and a superior zone. The boundaries between these zones are customer-driven and are shown as waves in order to indicate that they are based on the customers' perception of both what is required and what is delivered. This is to some extent subjective and varies according to the customer or even the mood of the customer.

In the deficient zone, the level of quality causes customers to complain, perhaps refuse to pay, or to return the product. They will probably not return or try the product again. This is definitely unacceptable, ultimately leading to disaster for the organization.

In the superior zone, the level of quality ensures satisfied customers who come back, bring their friends, and tell the supplier how much they like the product or service. The superior zone should be the target for every organization. It is a prerequisite for growth and prosperity.

In between lies the neutral zone, where the product or service is not bad enough for customers to complain but not good enough to ensure repeat business and referrals. You might be meeting the specification, even getting it right and on time. But is this enough?

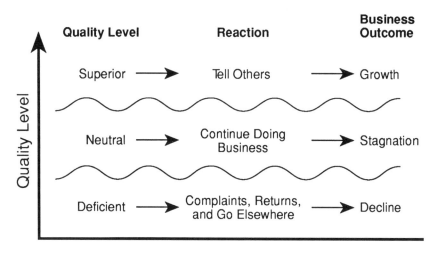

Figure 2.1   Quality Levels

To complicate matters, the boundary between the three levels of quality is not static. What was considered excellent yesterday will not suffice tomorrow. Standing still is really going backwards. Furthermore, the boundaries are influenced by your customers' experiences elsewhere, even in totally unrelated industries. A customer could emerge from a three-day visit to Disney World expecting the same high level of service and cleanliness in every other organization visited, yours included. And the ability of Federal Express to track a package anywhere in the world in minutes can make your customers impatient if you can't tell them when their order will be delivered without an "I'll get back to you this afternoon."

Quality is about meeting the needs and exceeding the expectations of customers. It is the route to growth, success, and in declining industries or periods of slow economic growth, survival.

Rather than attempt a precise or academic definition of quality, let's just say, "You know it when you see it," and more importantly, your customers know it when they see it. You can use ISO 9000 to make sure you deliver it and your customers "see it."

What is ISO 9000?

ISO 9000 is about management and satisfied customers—which means it is also about quality, and in particular, quality systems. ISO 9000 is a family of standards that define the requirements for an effective quality system. When an organization meets these requirements, it achieves ISO 9000 registration, indicating that its products or services are produced using certified processes.

The Standards are published by the International Organization for Standardization (IOS) based in Geneva, Switzerland, whose membership is made up of more than ninety countries. Independent national accreditation bodies in member countries accredit registrars who certify organizations to the ISO 9000 Standards. (Note: In Europe, Registrars are referred to as Certification Bodies.) ISO is not a scrambled acronym for the International Organization for Standardization. Instead, it comes from the Greek root, *isos*, meaning equal or uniform.

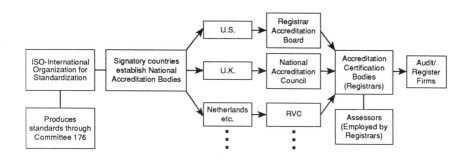

Figure 2.2   Certification Process

ISO 9000 Standards fall into two categories: Assessment Standards and Guidelines.

Assessment Standards

ISO 9001, 9002, and 9003 are the three assessment standards. All organizations, no matter their type or size, become registered to one of the three.

• ISO 9001 organizations provide products and services of their own design. Likely examples include: architects, software developers, and hard goods manufacturers.

• ISO 9002 is for organizations whose products and services are designed by someone else or by nature. Examples are: plating services, printers, nursing homes, and chemical plants. About two-thirds of registered organizations register to ISO 9002.

• ISO 9003, with only a small percentage of total registrations, is for organizations whose scope only involves final inspection and test. An example is a test laboratory.

15

Guidelines

Guidelines help organizations understand and apply the assessment standard to their businesses. ISO 9000-2 assists in determining which assessment standard is appropriate for an organization. The IOS divides businesses and organizations into four generic types, by product—hardware manufacturers, processed materials producers, service providers, and producers of software products.

Since the Standard was written by professionals in manufacturing, its language and orientation are geared to that audience. As shown in Figure 2.3, guideline documents exist for the other product types. ISO 9004-1 provides guidance for a more comprehensive quality system than the ISO 9000 assessment standards. It is sometimes referred to as a guideline for Total Quality Management.

Assessment Standards   **Guidelines**

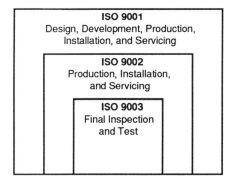

• 9000-1	Guidelines for the Selection and Use of ISO 9001, 9002, and 9003
• 9000-2	Guidelines for Application of ISO 9001, 9002, and 9003
• 9004-1	Quality Management and Quality System Elements
• 9004-2	Guidelines for Service
• 9004-3	Guidelines for Processed Materials
• 9000-3	Guidelines for Development, Supply, and Maintenance of Software
• 8402	Quality – Vocabulary

Figure 2.3   ISO 9000 Series of Standards

These guidelines, like the Standards themselves, are written by quality professionals for quality professionals. If you are not familiar with the terminology, you may find them hard to understand.

The ISO 9000 Quality System

Every organization has a quality system. This system is the way in which the organization identifies, defines, and meets the needs and expectations of its customers. The quality system is really the management system.

A quality system reflects the operation of the organization and its resources. It responds to changing needs, evolving as the organization evolves. Understanding the quality system and ensuring that it is optimal for the organization's needs is essential for its continued viability.

There is no such thing as a standard quality system because every organization is unique. Building a quality system can be compared to choosing a diet. There are five basic food groups and medical experts recommend that we consume food from each group every day to ensure that our bodies receive the minimum daily amounts of essential vitamins and minerals. We don't all like the same foods—some don't eat fish, others forego sweets. Fortunately, there are any number of foods from which we can choose and still meet our basic nutritional needs.

Similarly, there are different ways to satisfy the requirements of ISO 9000. The Standard allows many choices in building a quality system. You are not required to have a "standard" system—just a system that meets the Standard. As long as the basic requirements of the Standard are met, you can have any quality system you like.

The Standard is not extreme. Its requirements are minimal, but when properly understood and interpreted, they represent sound management. It is not surprising that most organizations already meet many of these requirements. If they didn't, they would be unable to meet the needs of their customers, and they would soon be out of business.

ISO 9000 Standards outline the requirements for quality management systems. Their purpose is to reduce, eliminate, and most importantly, prevent quality deficiencies. The Standard addresses quality systems, not product or service quality. The assumption is that an ISO 9000-compliant quality system will produce goods and services that increasingly satisfy or exceed the needs of the organization's customers.

The quality system is the control mechanism that ensures that all necessary activities are done. To achieve registration to an ISO 9000 assessment standard, an organization has to document its quality system, define how it will operate and control its operations, and then operate the business as documented.

The Facts of Life

This is a story about four people named Everybody, Somebody, Anybody, and Nobody. There was an important job to be done and Everybody was sure that Somebody would do it. Anybody could have done it, but Nobody did it. Somebody got angry about that, because it was Everybody's job. Everybody thought Anybody could do it, but Nobody realized that Everybody wouldn't do it. It ended up that Everybody blamed Somebody when Nobody did what Anybody could have done.

The way to change the "Facts of Life" is with structure, and the quality system is the basis of structure in an organization. It defines what is to be done, by whom, and when. It is the means by which the policy for quality is implemented. It defines the organization's strategy and tactics and ensures that its employees work together as a coordinated team.

What is in the Standard?

Appendix A is a questionnaire on the requirements of ISO 9001. By completing it, you can determine the extent to which your company complies with the Standard. Most organizations we have worked with were already satisfying many of the Standard's requirements—sometimes as many as 80% of them. In Appendix B there is a detailed explanation of the contents of the Standard. The meaning of the content is also defined and clarified.

ISO 9000—Where and How it Fits

We are often asked to compare ISO 9000 to Total Quality or Total Quality Management (TQM). They are not the same. Total Quality is a program or philosophy defined by an individual organization; therefore, it has no standard or common definition. TQM organizations generally:

- focus on customers (internal and external),
- require management leadership,
- involve employees,
- use data for decisions,
- determine customer needs to develop products, and
- plan for quality.

ISO 9000 is more concerned about effective outcomes than how things are done. Its aim is to ensure that registered firms give their customers what they want when they want it. With ISO 9000, you define a quality system to accomplish this and then demonstrate that you are using the system effectively to ensure quality.

ISO 9000 demands standardization and consistency. It requires that you find the optimum way to operate and consistently use that way until a better way is found. Many quality experts understand that standardization is necessary before big gains are made with Total Quality. Thus, ISO 9000 is a platform, or foundation, upon which an organization can further Total Quality Management. Figure 2.4 illustrates the relationship.

ISO 9000—The Future

ISO 9000 will be a part of your future. It will survive and continue to grow because it makes sense and because the global economy requires such standards and assessments. ISO 9000 also provides efficiencies in the customer-supplier interface. In the future, ISO 9000 registration will be a requirement for doing business in many industries. Large manufacturers understand this and are already requesting that their suppliers become registered. Industry groups and government agencies are adopting ISO 9000 for the same reason.

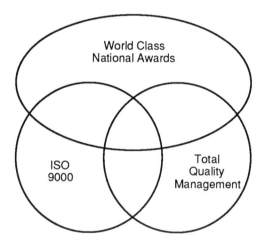

Figure 2.4   Quality Hierarchy

ISO 9000 provides a common standard and assessment scheme that facilitates international commerce. The International Organization for Standardization is currently working toward worldwide standardization of the accreditation processes and requirements. In the future, the training requirements for auditors, the prerequisites for assessment firms, and the accrediting processes and requirements will be recognized as the same everywhere. This universality will speed worldwide acceptance and use of the Standards and ensure their future.

Why Get Registered?

Today, the main reason for seeking ISO 9000 registration is market-related. Customers desire, expect, or require it, or a competitive market advantage is sought. But ISO 9000 registration can also provide operating benefits. Surveys of registered organizations indicate annual operating improvements of 3% to 5% of sales, with many organizations reporting even more substantial improvements.

A survey of the first 1,679 North American locations registered to ISO 9000 brought 720 responses, which ranked the following as the top four reasons for getting registered (Quality Systems Update, Fall, 1993 by CEEM Inc., Fairfax, Virginia):

- customer demands/expectations,
- quality benefits,
- market advantage, and
- requirements of European Community regulations.

Organizations seek ISO 9000 registration to give themselves an advantage over their competitors or to nullify the disadvantages when competitors are registered. We have worked with a number of organizations that were only going through the motions—until they learned that a competitor was seeking registration or that potential customers wanted to know if they were registered.

Benefits of Registration

The 720 survey respondents cited the benefits of ISO 9000 registration as:

External Benefits:

- higher perceived quality,
- improved customer satisfaction,
- competitive edge, and
- fewer customer quality audits.

Internal Benefits
- better documentation,
- greater quality awareness,
- positive "cultural" change, and
- increased operational efficiency/productivity.

Our research of CEOs of registered companies reveals significant positive changes in management and work force attitudes toward quality, reductions in quality costs, and increased company-wide acceptance of quality.

In a sense, getting registered is somewhat like being examined by a doctor. The exam itself doesn't make you better, but it tells you what you need to change and improve. ISO 9000 provides the mechanism for improving the business through its internal audit, management review, and corrective and preventive action requirements. This process is illustrated in Figure 2.5.

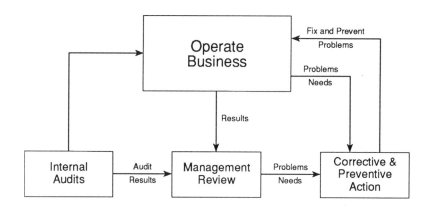

Figure 2.5   Improvement Loop

ISO 9000 is about improving the system, and that includes improving processes, work force, management, tools—everything. Most of our clients comment on the improvements in their company's management, and for many of them this is an unexpected bonus. They had envisioned a bureaucratic paper exercise.

When you approach ISO 9000 with a high level of commitment and a determination to get the most out of the project, you can expect many benefits. If you treat it as an imposed necessity or dump it on the quality department and keep your distance, registration may be achieved, but there will be few other rewards. The benefits from ISO 9000 are discussed in Chapter Three.

What is Involved?

Over the years we have heard just about everything—that achieving registration has taken from two months to several years and has cost from a few thousand dollars to several million. We believe all we've heard—each organization starts at a different point, counts differently, and approaches ISO 9000 differently.

What is Involved in Getting Registered?

In order to achieve ISO 9000 registration, you must demonstrate to the registrar during your audit that:

1. your documented quality system complies with the requirements of the appropriate Standard to which you are being registered,
2. you have implemented and are using that quality system as documented, and
3. your system is effective in controlling quality and supports the organization's quality policy and objectives.

These requirements translate into four major phases of registration:

A. analyze and evaluate the existing processes,
B. optimize and document the quality system,
C. implement, operate, and refine the quality system, and
D. registrar audit and registration.

The details of these phases are covered in Chapter 6. Phases A and B require the most work. There is even work to do for organizations with documented quality systems that comply with customer, military, or industry standards. These systems do not have the breadth of ISO 9000. They don't require internal auditing and management review and they don't cover the sales and product development functions. The expanded scope of ISO 9000 means adding and revising documents and, if there is an existing quality manual, rewriting it as well.

Phase C requires operating the business as documented and generating records showing the use and effectiveness of the system. In addition, it requires starting new activities such as internal audits, management reviews, and strict document control.

Phase D is the successful audit. If you do what's necessary in the first three phases, and show management commitment, you will not have a major noncompliance to deny or postpone registration. You can, however, expect minor noncompliances which can be easily cleared. The questionnaire in Appendix A will help determine your readiness for registration prior to the registrar's audit.

Documented Quality System

The biggest job in the registration process is documenting the quality system. The scheme in Figure 2.6 has evolved as best practice, and the ISO 9000 registrar will expect yours to be similar.

Level 1 - Quality Manual

A quality manual must define and explain:
- the organization's quality policy,
- how the requirements of the Standard are met, and
- the relationship between the quality system and the ISO 9000 Standard.

Quality manuals are typically between ten and twenty-five pages long and are best organized by section of the assessment standard. Because the quality manual defines the quality system, the ideal time to write it is after the rest of the quality system (Levels 2 and 3) has been satisfactorily completed.

The quality manual is not needed for internal operations. Many ISO 9000 companies include general information about the organization in their quality manuals and use them for marketing.

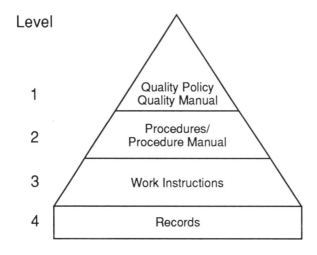

Level	Document	Addresses	Purpose	Responsibility
1	Quality Manual	Why	Policy	Executive Management
2	Procedures	Who, What, Where, When	Strategy	Management
3	Work Instructions	How	Tactics	Departments
4	Records	Effectiveness	Record of Performance	Everyone

Figure 2.6   Documentation Hierarchy

Level 2 - Procedures

Procedures define the "who, what, when, and where" of an organization's operations and are the heart of the quality system. Between ten and twenty-five procedures are usually needed to describe a quality system. Procedures should have a common format and are generally three to six pages long. See Appendix D (on pages 172–173) for a list of quality system procedures for typical service and manufacturing firms. Appendix E (beginning on page 174) is a sample procedure.

Level 3 - Work Instructions

Work Instructions describe how to complete tasks. They include operating instructions, engineering drawings, standards, and specifications. Because a common format is not required, existing work instructions need not be rewritten. ISO 9000 requires written work instructions only where their absence would adversely affect quality. An experienced and trained work force reduces the need for work instructions.

Level 4 - Records

Records are generated in the operation of a quality system and provide evidence that the system is operating and effective. Records may be computer-based or hard copy. Either way, they must be retrievable and kept until no longer needed.

Time Required for Registration

To understand the time required for ISO 9000 registration, we must separate the phases. Phases A and B together take from three to eight months to complete, with special situations outside this range. Several factors impact the time required:

- number of operating changes necessary to create a compliant and optimum system,

- number of new work instructions,
- available resources, both internal and external, and
- management's time objective.

Chapter 4 discusses the strategies and organization for becoming registered and the use of outside resources.

The time to complete Phase C, "Implement, Operate, and Refine the Quality System," is more easily definable. In this phase, you will need to work the "wrinkles" out of your system and generate records showing that the system works as it should.

Four to six months is usually sufficient time to demonstrate a working and effective quality system. During that period, registrars expect at least two rounds of internal audits and two management reviews. In practice, there is overlap between Phases A and B and Phase C.

In summary, the time range for getting registered is:

Phase A and B	3 - 8 months
Phase C	4 - 6 months
TOTAL TIME	7 - 14 months

The average time for our first 100 clients to achieve registration was seven months.

Cost of Registration

The cost of registration depends primarily on the size and complexity of the organization, its approach to registration, and its use of outside resources. Cost also depends on how an organization counts. Some count only external expenditures, while others include employee time and expenses.

The major costs are training, consulting assistance, employee time, and registrar fees. Successfully-operating businesses usually have no need to procure new equipment. There are some miscellaneous expenses for supplies and forms.

Equipment Expenses

The only essential equipment requirement is a word processor and printer, which almost everyone already has. The documentation phase involves drafting, reviewing, redrafting, and approving many documents, and efficient word processing is a must. New forms can be designed and reproduced within the company.

A potential expenditure is satisfying the calibration requirement. All measurements that determine and affect the quality of a product or service must be made with calibrated equipment. Organizations may have to invest in calibration services or equipment.

Training Expenses

Chapter 4 discusses training needs and alternatives. If your organization is not hiring a consultant, at least one employee needs to learn the Standard's requirements and be trained to design and document a compliant quality system. One or two courses totaling five days of training should be sufficient. In addition, internal auditors need to be trained, and all employees need awareness and job-specific training. You can easily estimate your training cost when you know the number of people to be trained, travel requirements, and course fees. If you want to train more than a few employees, a private class, tailored to your needs, may be the most cost-effective.

Consulting Assistance

Outside consultants can provide assistance in all phases of implementation. They can:

Phase A: Analyze and evaluate existing processes:

- provide training,

- evaluate existing processes, and

- reengineer processes.

Phase B: Optimize and document the quality system:

- provide guidance on optimizing processes,

- provide guidance on the Standard's requirements, and

- write some of the documentation.

Phase C: Implement, operate, refine the quality system:

- provide guidance,

- train the internal auditing team, and

- determine the readiness of the organization for its registrar audit.

Phase D: Registrar audit and registration

- provide guidance during the audit and in clearing noncompliances found during the audit.

During Phase D, a consultant's role is behind the scenes. Some registrars refuse to speak to consultants during an audit. They want to be sure that the quality system is the organization's and that the employees know the system and can operate it.

> *Many of the organizations we have helped wanted all of the above assistance, including our taking the lead in documenting their quality system. The companies had from 2 to 2,500 employees, and our fees ranged from $10,000 to $25,000. (Comparable figures in the United Kingdom are £4,000 to £15,000.) Fees for organizations involving multiple locations are higher.*

Employee Time

Employee time is inversely related to consulting assistance. At one extreme you can hire a consultant to analyze and document the entire quality system. At the other extreme your implementation team can be trained to complete phases A and B on their own. Or you can opt for something in between.

Given the time, most engineers could design and build their own homes and maintain their own cars. But most decide this is not an optimum use of their time, and so they hire experts to do the work. Growing businesses and businesses with limited staff may approach ISO 9000 registration the same way.

Determining how much employee time is spent on Phase C is difficult because using your quality system *is* operating the business, and you do that anyway. When you reach the registration audit, employees will be meeting with the auditors, accompanying the auditors, making changes, and responding to auditor requests.

Our experience has shown that during the registration process, organizations of 50 to 1,000 employees usually need the following amounts of employee time over the duration of the project:

Less than 100 employees	50 - 100	person-days
101 - 500 employees	75 - 150	person-days
Over 500 employees	100 - 200	person-days

These times are typical of companies making a sustained and well-organized effort. They apply to team members directly working on the project. The time for general training, management and project review meetings, and communication is not included.

Registrar Fees

Registrar fees are quite easy to determine. When requested, registrars send out promotional information and questionnaire/ application forms. Based on the information you provide—the size of your company, number of locations, number of employees, and the appropriate ISO 9000 Standard—registrars provide firm quotes. These quotes cover the audit and registration, optional pre-assessment audits, and surveillance audits.

Registrar fees for the initial audit and registration of a single location can be estimated as in the example on the next page.

NORTH AMERICA

Employees	9001	9002
Less than 30	$7,000 - $ 9,000	$6,000 - $8,000
30 to 100	8,000 - 11,000	7,000 - 10,000
100 to 500	11,000 - 19,000	8,000 - 16,000
500 to 1,000	15,000 - 24,000	10,000 - 20,000

UNITED KINGDOM

Employees	9001	9002
Less than 30	£1,500 - £3,000	£1,300 - £2,500
30 to 100	2,000 - 3,500	1,800 - 3,000
100 to 500	2,800 - 5,000	2,500 - 4,500
500 to 1,000	3,500 - 7,000	3,000 - 6,000

Note: Auditor travel expenses are not included.

The above estimates are general. Price quotations should be obtained to determine the actual costs to your business. In some instances, travel can add a significant amount to the total cost of registration. Because registrars have different registration periods and approaches to re-registration and surveillance audits, you should estimate the total cost over a five year time frame for comparison purposes.

ISO 9000 - Your Decision

How do you decide whether ISO 9000 registration is right for your organization? For some, the decision has already been made—the market requires their registration. But for others, it is not so easy—their decision needs to be justified.

When considering ISO 9000 registration, managers usually don't think about maximizing the benefits and the return on investment (which may have been considerable). We mention those potential returns here to emphasize that *there is far more to be gained from ISO 9000 registration than a certificate for the wall.* This chapter presents tangibles—some costs and some benefits. But there are intangibles and non-quantifiable benefits as well. Our research and experience indicate that with ISO 9000 registration, the *intangibles* are a major factor.

What is the value of being perceived as a high-quality organization? Employees of registered organizations are much more aware of and concerned with quality issues than those of non-registered organizations. How do you place a value on this?

> *A large manufacturer became registered to ISO 9000 two years after it had received the Malcolm Baldrige Quality Award. Company insiders reported more employee pride and a greater sense of accomplishment from the ISO 9000 registration. ISO 9000 involved more employees and had a greater impact on their jobs. In contrast, the Baldrige award was primarily viewed as a management accomplishment. Employee pride is bound to translate into tangible benefits, but how do you measure pride?*

Some executives say they plan to get registered "but not right now." The registration process is a major project, and there may be legitimate reasons for waiting. Other executives are waiting to see if ISO 9000 is just another fad. We believe they are making a mistake. ISO 9000 makes too much sense in a global economy to be a fad. In the United Kingdom, where the Standard has been used for over fifteen years, data support the forecasts that ISO 9000 will be a business and competitive factor for a long, long time.

Summary

Once you decide that you want your organization registered, you need to determine how to accomplish that objective. We hope you find this book useful. We encourage you to *look beyond regis-*

tration. Reach for and realize the additional benefits your achievement can bring. The remainder of this book offers our approach to ISO 9000. It facilitates registration and, more importantly, gives you a quality system that is sure to improve your business. We are convinced that ISO 9000, done right, is a good investment. This book is about "doing it right" and maximizing your return.

The following chapter discusses in more detail all of the benefits ISO 9000 can bring. Together, these two chapters provide input for you to make an informed decision about ISO 9000 registration for your organization. Chapters 4 and 5 describe how management can maximize the benefits of ISO 9000.

When you decide to pursue ISO 9000 registration, you are committing a substantial investment of resources. You will want to maximize the benefits you receive from that investment. This chapter alerts you to the potential benefits of ISO 9000. The remainder of the book explains how to realize them.

Typically, registered firms cite marketing and operating benefits from registration. These are discussed. Benefits are also attainable while pursuing registration. And further benefits reach beyond the registration certificate for long-term gains. This chapter discusses benefits during three periods:

- Implementing ISO 9000
- Registration
- Beyond ISO 9000 Registration

Chapter 3

The ISO 9000 Pay-Back

In This Chapter:

- Benefits of ISO 9000—the typical and not so obvious
- Benefits before and after registration
- Exploiting ISO 9000 registration for market advantage
- Using ISO 9000 for continual improvement
- Operating improvements from ISO 9000 registration
- ISO 9000 and your organization
- Reengineering processes
- If ISO works for part of the organization, why not for the rest?
- ISO 9000 as a platform for Total Quality
- From ISO 9000 to Process Management

ISO 9000 has the potential to substantially impact an organization. Its significance is enough to bring dramatic changes. The purpose of this book is to show how ISO 9000 can impact an organization and how to realize the benefits. Some benefits just happen. For example, an ISO 9000 registration certificate will open up certain markets. Other benefits must be sought and accrued through careful planning and determination.

Organizations can begin accruing benefits during the implementation phase. ISO 9000 registration requires documentation of the quality system. This is an ideal opportunity to examine how the organization functions and make changes to improve the system and operation of the business.

Some benefits occur after the registration certificate is received. Marketing advantages can be exploited. The improved quality system yields improved operating efficiencies—a big advantage. ISO 9000 can be a stepping stone to Total Quality, process management, and improvements of non-ISO 9000 areas in the organization.

The discussion of benefits in this chapter is organized by project stage: Implementing ISO 9000, Registration, and Beyond ISO 9000 Registration.

Implementing ISO 9000
- Improvement
- Reengineering

Registration
- Market Advantage
- Continual Improvement
- Fewer "Fires"
- Quality Culture
- Supplier Management

Beyond ISO 9000 Registration
- Total Company
- Total Quality Management
- Process Management

Implementing ISO 9000

The Process Management Approach to ISO 9000 registration starts with the identification of key processes. These processes are the basis of the procedures that constitute the quality system. Before documenting your quality system, examine your processes to make sure they meet your objectives, meet the requirements of the Standard, and above all, are right for your business. If they are not, they need to be changed before documentation. Don't just document what you do. *Evaluate and improve what you do,* and then document it. Maybe reengineering—a more dramatic analysis and change—is in order. Figure 3.1 provides a flow chart of the activities at this stage.

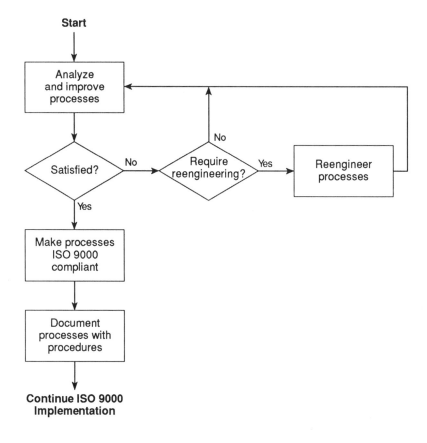

Figure 3.1   Process Improvement

Improvements

The Process Management Approach to ISO 9000, discussed in the next chapter, starts with what you do now. Some changes will always be necessary to comply with the Standard. You must analyze existing processes for compliance to the Standard. These analyses will yield changes and improvements that will improve performance. Most organizations know what and where they need to improve but, for some reason, don't take the time to make the changes. ISO 9000 registration is the time to make improvements. It is important to make changes, big or small, before the system is documented.

> *A client already had a calibration program that complied with ISO 9000 requirements. All measuring equipment was calibrated every three months. As they were writing the calibration procedure, someone asked, "Why are we calibrating quarterly?" Good question. Calibration was costly because much of the work was done by a calibration service.*
>
> *An analysis of operating data indicated no need for such frequent calibration, nor did the manufacturers' recommendations. So the client reduced the frequency of calibration to between six months and a year and realized a huge annual savings with no adverse impact on quality.*

Reengineering

Reengineering takes improvement further than incremental change. Here you discard the old rules and reasons for doing things and ask, "Why are we doing this at all?" You start with a clean slate and explore different ways to achieve objectives. The results can be radically different ways of working and new views of your organization's structure, jobs, and roles.

These new views are ideals—visions of where you would like to be. There may be good reasons why you cannot implement them now, but this does not invalidate the reengineering approach. Without such visions, there would be nothing to aim for. The reality, the changes you do implement, may be the optimum solution for now.

Preparing for registration may be the opportunity to reengineer processes identified as important but "underachieving." If you are not competitive using existing processes, make the necessary changes before documenting for ISO 9000 registration.

Registration

Registration brings its rewards. The main reason organizations today seek ISO 9000 registration is market-related. Either they are seeking a competitive advantage in their market and see this as an opportunity to differentiate themselves; they are playing catch-up; or their customers desire, expect, and/or require their registration. But ISO 9000 registration can and should provide more than just marketing benefits. Surveys of registered organizations show annual operating improvements as well—some as high as 50% in important operating parameters. This section covers some "typical" benefits from the registration and resulting quality system.

Market Advantage

A few years ago, it was widely believed that ISO 9000 registration was required to sell products in the European Community. That belief was only partially correct and impacted only a small percentage of organizations pursuing ISO 9000 registration. Now ISO 9000 is fast becoming a requirement for doing business in all markets—local, state, and national, as well as international. *Customers are the driving force behind ISO 9000's growth.*

> *An international corporation registered two manufacturing plants to ISO 9000. The initiative for the effort came from the plants themselves. When we saw the corporation's glossy quality manual, we assumed it was used as a sales piece. So we visited*

39

their main sales office, located within 10 miles of the registered plants, to see how the sales department was capitalizing on the ISO 9000 investment. It wasn't! In fact, the employees in the sales office only vaguely recalled hearing about ISO 9000 and had no understanding of what it was or how it could impact the business.

This scenario is easily explained. The company's market did not require or even know about ISO 9000, but the management realized that the Standard was valuable in its own right. As ISO 9000 becomes a factor in more industries, such a scenario will become as rare as a buggy whip.

Once registered, organizations need to exploit their registration. They need to advertise to "spread the word" and gain market advantage. When you get registered, publicize it! Teach the sales force and other employees how ISO 9000 registration differentiates the organization. Use registration logos on sales literature and stationery. This tells customers and potential customers about your achievement and commitment to quality.

Press releases are effective and economical. One should go to the trade press in order to notify customers, prospects, and competitors. A second press release to the local paper lets the community know of your accomplishment. Your employees will be proud to be recognized by their neighbors as part of a quality organization.

Continual Improvement

If registration to the ISO 9000 Standard does not result in improvements to your business, something is wrong. In the United Kingdom, where the Standard has been most widely applied, surveys indicate that most firms, both service and manufacturing, enjoy increased productivity. Even small firms report 5% and higher operating improvements as a percent of sales. In addition, they show improvements in operating parameters such as order turnaround, scrap, and overtime.

ISO 9000 requires an organization to track important quality indicators. It must document and take action on customer complaints, product returns, internal nonconformances, supplier difficulties, and other measures important to the business. All of these are reviewed by management and action taken to eliminate their causes. Using the ISO 9000 requirements to establish an effective continual improvement process is the best opportunity for return on investment. Internal audits, management reviews, and corrective and preventive actions are requirements of the Standard. Figure 3.2 illustrates the ISO 9000 continual improvement process.

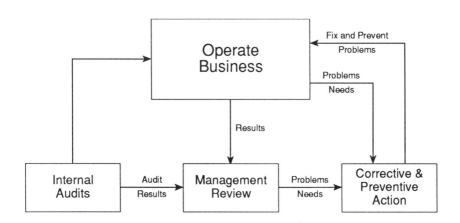

Figure 3.2   The ISO 9000 System Improvement Loop

Management reviews and internal audits, both required by ISO 9000, uncover existing and potential problems. How the organization reacts to this information makes the difference between good and "so-so" improvement. Employees should not be defensive but instead see problems as opportunities for improvement. ISO 9000 is about improving the system, and that includes everything—processes, tools, management, products, and the work force. When executive management approaches ISO 9000 registration with a high level of commitment and a determination to get the most out of the project, the benefits are many. But if registration is seen only as an imposed necessity, there will be few other rewards. Real improvements and real solutions bring real gains.

A major role for executive management is the management review. *How these reviews are positioned and conducted greatly influences the level of improvement.* While the reviews are required, the agenda for them is left to management—and management review meetings can address any subject. But to effectively improve processes, these meetings *must* address and reduce external customer dissatisfaction and negative internal performance such as complaints, returns, scrap, rework, downtime, defects, and warranty costs. If management takes the reviews seriously and uses them to improve processes and solve problems, gains will be realized.

Problems need to be identified and reviewed, and then, action must be taken to eliminate them. Problem solving actions fall into three categories:

- Remedial action: fixes the symptom(s),
- Corrective action: corrects the cause(s),
- Preventive action: uses knowledge of the problem to reduce or prevent similar occurrences in the immediate product and elsewhere.

A good action fixes the cause of a problem and prevents it from recurring in that particular and similar situations. For example, it might be discovered during assembly that two adjacent parts from different suppliers are not painted exactly the same color. The first solution can be to repaint one item to match the other. That is a remedial action. Another solution can be to contact the suppliers to ensure that they use the same color of paint—a corrective action. A third possibility is a policy where all mating parts are painted in contrasting colors or painted by the same supplier. This is a preventive action.

Taking internal audits, management review, and corrective and preventive action seriously provides the mechanism and discipline for continual improvement.

Fewer "Fires"

A documented quality system promotes communication, coordination, and alignment of activities. Problems are reduced by increased control, standardization, and improved employee understanding, coordination, and involvement. The quality system promotes consistency in how work is done and recorded. It helps new employees learn more easily and quickly what should be done. A documented quality system is a good tool for training both new and current employees.

ISO 9000 also reduces misunderstandings with customers by formally connecting the two with a contract or purchase agreement. Before signing the agreement, the seller must confirm that it has the capability to fulfill the agreement. This requirement increases the likelihood of a satisfied customer.

All of these factors contribute to a smoother-running operation with fewer crises and "fires" to work on. More time can then be spent improving the business and satisfying its customers.

Quality Culture

By the time an organization is registered, its employees will have heard about ISO 9000 many times. They are continually reminded of ISO 9000 through internal audits, quality system documents, registrar audits, and the changes resulting from ISO 9000 registration. Communication is particularly important throughout the implementation phase, and the recurring message should be that ISO 9000 is about improving the organization and exceeding the needs of customers. That message needs to continue after registration is attained.

ISO 9000 is not a one-shot deal in which an organization gets registered and then forgets it. The organization must be periodically audited by its registrar, continually audit itself, review the operation and suitability of its systems, identify problems, and seek solutions.

ISO 9000 registration raises the quality awareness and customer consciousness levels of all employees. It is management's job to maintain and build on these beneficial side effects of registration. Management should communicate and reinforce quality awareness, customer consciousness, and other desirable values until they become part of the organization's culture.

Supplier Management

Companies, especially larger ones, can use ISO 9000 to reduce the cost of their supplier management programs. They now spend considerable sums to develop supplier standards and to verify compliance to these standards. And the suppliers are forced to comply with different requirements and audits from different customers. The system is highly redundant, inefficient, and expensive. In the late 1970s the British developed the BS 5750 Standards and a third-party assessment scheme to eliminate these inefficiencies. Those standards were the beginning of ISO 9000.

> *When large manufacturers in the U.S. want assurance of quality from suppliers, they impose their own standards on the suppliers and audit them for compliance. Suppliers with several customers have to comply with the various quality systems. So it has been in the United States automobile industry.*
>
> *Auto industry suppliers knew there had to be a better way and requested that the big auto makers adopt common quality requirements. In late 1993 the auto industry agreed to adopt a common system and chose ISO 9000 as the Standard. Efficiencies will be realized by both suppliers and car makers. It is hoped ISO 9000, the common Standard, will turn a tenuous relationship into one that benefits all parties.*

Summary

The benefits in this section—market advantage, continual improvement, fewer fires, and improved culture—are those most often attributed to ISO 9000 by registered firms. But not all organizations see these benefits—they don't arrive with the certificate. Management must make sure they occur. Management can use ISO 9000 to change its culture and improve operations. Management can exploit registration in its markets. And there is more. ISO 9000 can be the foundation for achieving still higher levels of performance by looking beyond the basic requirements of registration.

Beyond ISO 9000 Registration

Unfortunately, many organizations approach ISO 9000 as a burden they must endure and try to become registered with minimum effort. If they manage to avoid implementing an inefficient and bureaucratic system, they may realize some of the above-mentioned benefits. But most miss the biggest potential benefits. These benefits don't just happen. Management must go beyond the minimum ISO 9000 registration to realize them. This is achieved by applying the principles of ISO 9000 to all functions of the organization, embracing Total Quality Management, and keeping a process management perspective.

The Total Company

ISO 9000 does not cover all of the key processes and functions of a business. Accounting, for instance, is not included in the ISO 9000 Standards, even though invoicing errors can negatively impact the customer relationship. Other functions not covered by ISO 9000 are human resources, security, and finance.

Most registered organizations don't interpret the Standards to include critical processes like determining customer needs, pre-sales

45

activities, planning, and determining customer satisfaction. Yet these processes are all vital to the success of the organization. Proximity to the customer is the main distinction between processes and functions covered or not covered by ISO 9000. The Standard's concern is that an organization's external customers are content with the products and services they receive. Hence the ISO 9000 focus is on core processes that identify, design, provide and deliver products and services. The excluded functions and processes support the core processes.

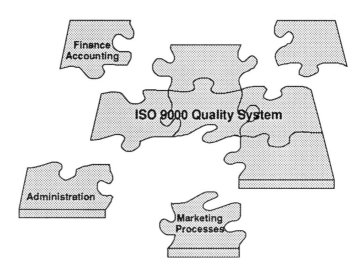

Figure 3.3   ISO 9000 and the Total Company

Management must determine if the excluded functions and processes can be improved by ISO 9000. If registration brings order, standardization of best practices, consistency, and efficiency to the covered processes, it only makes sense to extend coverage to the rest of the organization. In expanding ISO 9000 coverage, the organization defines the requirements for the newly covered areas.

It can arrange for an ISO 9000 audit to cover the expanded scope. Otherwise, the registrar auditors will only audit to the scope of the Standard.

This quality system extension can either be incorporated into the overall quality system of the organization or remain separate. Activities such as internal auditing and management review can obviously benefit all of the organization. Other ISO 9000-type requirements such as contract review, document control, and corrective and preventive action will certainly apply to the expanded scope. Because the current quality policy may not be applicable to all support functions, their managers can define their own quality policies and objectives, identify their customers' needs and expectations, and document systems that enable them to meet the requirements of their customers.

The Standard's contract review requirement provides a good opportunity for managers to sit down and, often for the first time, define the services provided by various departments, such as accounting or personnel. Thinking in terms of a supplier-customer relationship, and defining the service as if it were a transaction with an outside supplier, can be productive. Some organizations go even further by registering additional functions independently.

One client, a multi-plant business, registered its headquarters function that included central purchasing and support for the organization's production/distribution centers. The production/distribution centers were registered separately.

Functions to be registered define the scope of their registration by the services they provide and are assessed against the appropriate ISO 9000 Standard.

We have also seen where expanded registration has changed the mission of an internal function.

A large international corporation only used its residential conference facility for internal training. Low utilization and uneven

47

demand played havoc with the conference center, which was trying to operate efficiently. Although the conference center was not included in the corporation's ISO 9000 registration, it embraced the Standard as a means for improving its operation. This led to a separate ISO 9000 registration, which in turn, led to offering the facility and catering services to outside organizations. The extra business increased the utilization and operating efficiency of the conference facility, absorbed more overhead, and reduced operating costs.

As ISO 9000 evolves, it will certainly expand in scope and requirements. Functions and processes not covered now may soon become part of a future Standard. But many organizations are not waiting. For them, documenting, analyzing, and improving processes—all required by ISO 9000 Standards—make sense for every part of the organization today.

A world-renown registrar from the United Kingdom, the British Standards Institute, is formally registering organizations under a company-wide registration plan. The plan and registration cover organizations in their entirety. We don't yet know if this will become a trend, but we do know that extending the registration process to the entire organization makes sense.

Total Quality Management (TQM)

Is ISO 9000 the same as Total Quality Management? If not, are they compatible? If I am doing TQM, do I need ISO 9000? And vice versa?

We touched on some of the answers in Chapter Two: "ISO 9000 - Where and How it Fits" (page 19). ISO 9000 and TQM are not the same, but they are compatible. ISO 9000 is a strong foundation for TQM, which goes beyond the Standard (see Figure 3.4). The purpose they share is to satisfy customers and continually improve processes. Both require management leadership and management involvement. ISO 9000 and TQM actually reinforce each other, and both are needed.

Still, ISO 9000 and TQM have different means to accomplish their objectives. ISO 9000 requires that an organization develop a quality system and then use it to accomplish its goal of satisfying customers. To do this, an organization must examine, standardize, and document its processes. Employees understand what needs to be done, and the quality system ensures that activities are carried out consistently. ISO 9000 provides a mechanism for continual improvement.

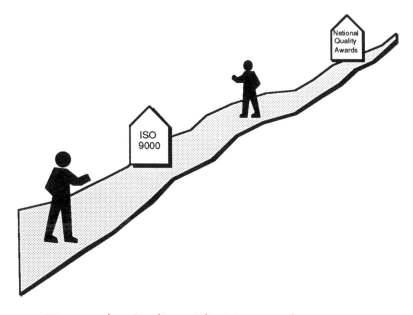

Figure 3.4   Quality...The Never-Ending Journey

Total Quality is not regulated by an overall standard but is a concept that varies with each organization. Company, state, industry, and national quality award programs are sometimes used as "standards." These programs, including the Malcolm Baldrige Quality Award in the U.S., have differing criteria that define a "quality" organization. Recipients of national awards are designated as "world-class quality organizations."

When the Malcolm Baldrige criteria are used as the Standard for TQM, differences between Total Quality and ISO 9000 are apparent. The main differences are:

- Employee involvement: ISO 9000 does not specify involvement, but it is a necessity. ISO 9000 requires a qualified work force, and that involves training. Total Quality, as defined by the Baldrige criteria, demands employee involvement. The Baldrige criteria look for evidence that an organization is fully utilizing its human resources. They address training, empowerment, participation, and reward systems.

- Quality Planning: ISO 9000 refers to quality planning in the context of manufacturing products and delivering services. Baldrige has a broader view of quality, expecting it to be given the highest priority and attention. Baldrige examines and evaluates how effective the organization is in achieving and retaining quality leadership.

- Measurement and Results: ISO 9000 requires an effective quality system that produces conforming products and satisfied customers. Baldrige wants to know which measures and indicators, internal as well as customer-based, are important and desires that the data on these measures be benchmarked against industry and world-class organizations. The comparisons must be favorable and the data must improve over time. Analysis of such data is important to Baldrige.

- Processes: ISO 9000 requires documenting key processes. Baldrige requires effective processes for developing products and services that meet and exceed the needs of customers. This is the area where the two overlap the most and where ISO 9000 "scores points" in a Baldrige evaluation.

Future revisions of the ISO 9000 Standard will incorporate more features commonly associated with TQM. Just as the recent revision increased requirements for corrective and preventive action, the next revision will likely address involvement of the work force. Even now, registrar auditors want to see evidence of fact-based problem-solving—a characteristic of Total Quality Management.

Figure 3.5 illustrates how ISO 9000 and Total Quality can impact an organization. ISO 9000 by itself brings stability, consistency, and improved performance. It reduces the "fires" that are so unproductive and demand so much of every one's time. ISO 9000 also provides a base on which to further improve the business. Total Quality can provide the improvements.

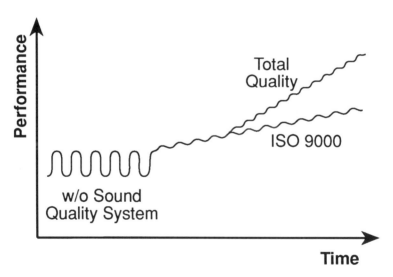

Figure 3.5   Organization Performance

Process Management

Process Management means viewing and operating an organization based on its key processes (see Figure 3.6). Process improvement is the improvement of the effectiveness and efficiency of these processes. Process innovation is making dramatic changes in how processes operate. ISO 9000 registration can be the beginning of process management, improvement, and innovation.

Most organizations are managed as if they were composed of distinct, independent functional units that, through meeting their defined objectives, collectively meet the organization's objectives. This has proven to be an inefficient approach that leads to suboptimization of the system. A better approach is to manage the organization as a system of processes.

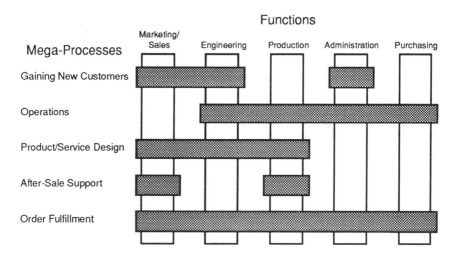

Figure 3.6   Process View of an Organization

Managing "by the organizational chart" inevitably leads to inefficiencies and suboptimization in which departmental goals are pursued to the possible detriment of the whole. Process management is a way to overcome suboptimization and lack of cooperation between departments. All activities need to align with the processes that provide value to the external customer. Through innovation and improvement of these key processes, impressive gains in efficiency and customer satisfaction are made.

A systems approach to management takes a holistic view of the organization, viewing it as a unified, purposeful system composed of interrelated processes. Instead of dealing separately with functional activities, the system is managed by a process hierarchy.

Organizations need to have a process orientation from the beginning. Document your quality system as a series of processes. Process management doesn't mean throwing out your functional organization. With a functional organization, you can still identify key processes and process owners. This orientation will let you manage and improve the process irrespective of functional entities.

Summary

Improvements don't stop with registration. Just because a quality system is documented and meets the requirements of the Standard does not mean it is carved in stone. Everyone needs to use the documented system to improve the management and performance of the business.

The following chapters detail management's role and the decisions managers must make in order to realize the benefits of ISO 9000. Use the discussion to set high expectations for ISO 9000. When management expects and plans for extra benefits, they will happen.

The benefits discussed in the last chapter are attainable only if management expects and plans for them. It is critical to become registered efficiently and with a quality system that benefits the business. Before starting to implement ISO 9000, important decisions need to be made. In this chapter we discuss those decisions and choices. We also introduce the Process Management Approach to ISO 9000 registration—which we have used to register more than 150 sites.

Chapter 4

Key Decisions

In This Chapter:

- Determining the scope of registration
- Developing an optimum quality system
- The Process Management Approach
- Setting objectives beyond registration
- Using outside assistance
- Internal resource requirements and how they are organized
- The optimum way to meet the internal auditing requirement
- Selecting and hiring a registrar
- Pre-assessment

Determining the Scope of the Registration

The Assessment Standard

Organizations are registered to one of the three ISO 9000 Assessment Standards—ISO 9001, 9002, or 9003. The Standards differ only by scope and are not an indicator of quality. ISO 9001 is the appropriate Standard for organizations that design products or services. Companies that produce to other organizations' specifications or whose products are fixed in nature, (*e.g.*, carbon dioxide), register to ISO 9002. ISO 9003 is for organizations that are only involved in final inspection and test. Chapter Two has additional information on the differences between the assessment standards.

To find the appropriate Standard for your organization, see Figure 4.1. It indicates that the scope of the business determines the appropriate Standard. But that is only one consideration. Others are location, business strategy, and economics.

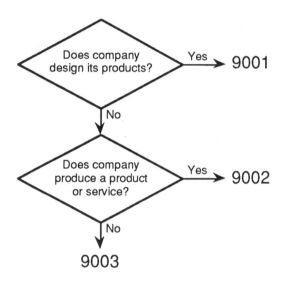

Figure 4.1   The Appropriate Standard

The Scope of the Registration

If the location to be registered does not contain a product design or development function, it is registered to ISO 9002 even when it is part of an organization that develops its own products. Organizations having a central design group and remote manufacturing facilities usually register the location with the design function to ISO 9001 and the manufacturing facilities to ISO 9002.

Most registrations are for a single facility or multiple facilities in close proximity. Yet some companies choose to register widely-dispersed sites under one registration. Although such an arrangement can mean big savings, especially in registrar fees, it may not be practical or optimal. Registering sites individually promotes local ownership and facilitates the ongoing operation and improvement of the quality system at each site.

One situation where a single registration for widely-scattered sites might be appropriate is when the sites are clones, operating under a central control system. In that case, the registrar may agree to initial registration by auditing a sample of sites, visiting those remaining during subsequent surveillance audits. Registrar fees would be much less than if each site were audited.

In addition to choice of Standard, you may also chose the areas of business that you want registered. You may register only some functions, *e.g.,* Manufacturing, even when Development is located in the same facility. This is not always a wise decision however. Your strategy may be to "start with Manufacturing and include Development later," but such a plan can send the wrong message to the market and to your employees. Exclusions raise questions about a company's commitment to quality. People ask, "Does this mean Product Development doesn't believe in quality?" or "Is Design out of control?" Some registrars will not work for organizations that want to register only part of the business unless there is good reason for the exclusion.

Companies also have the option of excluding certain product lines, but this too sends negative messages and raises questions. Yet there are situations where an exclusion is justified. For example, if a company is discontinuing certain lines or processes in the near future, bringing them up to standard now would not be worth the effort and expense. When certain products and services are excluded, it is imperative that customers and prospects not be misled. They must be told precisely what is and what is not covered by the registered quality system.

> *A car dealership decided to seek ISO 9000 registration—not for the entire organization, but just for its fleet operation. Only those processes involving sales to fleet customers were documented. The other parts of the dealership were treated like sub-contractors. Of the 90-plus employees, just three were involved in the fleet operation. That registration had a steep price— ninety employees who seriously doubted their employer's commitment to quality.*

Before hiring a registrar, get input from several as to which ISO 9000 Standard is appropriate for your company and what the scope of the registration should be. Their responses will not only increase your understanding of this aspect of the process; they will help you decide which registrar you want to hire.

> *When it became apparent during a registrar audit that Product Design would not meet the ISO 9001 Standard, the lead auditor suggested removing it from the scope of the audit. Once that was done, the auditor approved the organization's remaining activities for registration to ISO 9002. This registration was not only a farce; it also raised questions about the integrity of a registrar that would allow such practices.*

Developing the Optimum Quality System

The ideal quality system is one that adds value to the business and produces benefits beyond the certificate. There are plenty of "fly-by-night" types who will promise you just such a system—all you have to do is buy their product. Their ads claim that for £100 or $495 or $2,400, "this software program" or "that workbook" will give you a quality system that satisfies ISO 9000 Standards and more. These products sometimes lead to registration, but they will *never* produce an optimum, benefit-producing system. Your organization is unique, and it needs a unique quality system.

Shortly after the glow of registration fades, organizations using someone else's system learn their purchase is more a hindrance than a help. We have been sought out by registered companies that had foolishly taken this route. The usual plea is, "Give us a system we can live with," or "Help us develop a system that will help improve our business."

The Process Management Model

In our other book, *Achieving ISO 9000 Registration*, we detailed the Process Management Approach to ISO 9000 registration. This approach accomplishes registration efficiently and results in an optimum quality system. In general, the Process Management Approach:

- starts with the existing system,
- identifies and evaluates the business's processes,
- documents the processes with logically determined procedures,
- writes user-friendly procedures that describe what needs to be done and by whom,
- uses the terminology of the business, not of the Standard,
- does not over-document,
- involves employees in all phases of the implementation, and
- requires management leadership.

The approach starts with your present system, or *modus operandi*. If your organization is like most, it already satisfies a high percentage of the ISO 9000 requirements. Thus, it is only logical for you to continue what you now do. Remember, "If it ain't broke, don't fix it!" But if it is "broke," or if you are not happy with your current operation, make changes and additions for an improved operation while maintaining compliance with the Standard.

ISO 9000 Standards do not require that everything be documented, and the Process Management Approach reduces non-essential documentation—especially work instructions. The Standard says that written instructions are needed only where their absence would adversely affect quality. If your employees have managed to perform tasks without using work instructions, you are not required to write them for ISO 9000 registration. If you want to write work instructions, you are certainly free to do so, but it should be for reasons other than meeting the Standards of ISO 9000.

In the Process Management Approach, the documented quality system defines the organization's processes and the way the organization operates. Processes are logically defined without regard to either the standard boundaries or the boundaries of internal functions. This approach uses the same terminology you and your employees already use, which makes the documented operating procedures meaningful, understandable, and thus, more useful to your employees. When your employees read the procedures and their job titles, they immediately identify the system as theirs.

The procedures for a small automobile dealership are listed in Figure 4.2. Note that the terminology of the procedures reflects the dealership and not the Standard.

Selling	Delivering		Ensuring	
Sale of Cars	Service	Supplier Approval	Internal Auditing	Control of Computer Systems
Sale of Parts	Control of Parts	Inter-Dealer Trading	Management Review and Corrective Action	Specification Control
Sale of Finance	Control of Vehicles		Calibration	Customer Complaints
			Control of Non-Conforming Parts	

Figure 4.2   Processes and Procedures
for an Automobile Dealership

The Process Management Approach is straightforward and logical. Unfortunately, the same cannot be said for some other approaches. If you ever hear about "the awful experience" someone's organization had with ISO 9000, it is most likely that another approach had been tried and failed.

Two approaches, both less than optimal and both widely used, are described below. They are "Implementing Someone Else's System" and "Implementing the Standard."

Implementing Someone Else's System

In 1985, when we began working with clients seeking ISO 9000 registration, we tried to develop a common system to meet the documentation and compliance needs of all manufacturing companies. We believed that because they all sell, design, purchase, produce, and deliver products, a generic set of procedures could be developed for easy use by any one of them. We were naive.

The "canned systems" on the market in North America and Europe claim to be universally applicable to any organization. Purchasers are told to read the text, and where they see the words "any company," replace them with the name of their organization.

From discussions with registrars, we know that an organization can sometimes proceed as far as the registration audit using such documentation. But it soon becomes apparent to the auditors that no one in the company has any idea how the system operates with respect to the Standard, and the audit is aborted. What an incredible waste of resources!

Every organization is unique. Even if organizations perform the same general functions, they usually operate in different ways.

Two automobile dealerships, only ten miles apart, were owned by the same parent company and sold the same manufacturer's products. Yet they used widely different methods of operation and control. Why? Because they were different. They didn't have the

61

same management. They didn't have the same employees. They didn't have the same customers.

They were different organizations operating in different environments. A system and its environment interact. They codetermine one another. Any environment is unique, and the system determined by it will be unique.

An organization and its quality system evolve with time. The wholesale importation of a *foreign* quality system disrupts that environment and mitigates against successful operation. Such a system may lead to registration, but it will not improve the business. Rather it will alienate employees and make registration very difficult.

Do not start with someone else's system—whether it is purchased or "borrowed" from a neighboring company. No matter how tempting it looks or how similar the business may be to yours, the system is foreign. You must have your own system.

Amazingly, some organizations operate two parallel systems. They implement a foreign system for ISO 9000 and still operate their business using the old system. Not only is this extremely inefficient, it sounds like a horrendous task!

One of our clients, a large designer and manufacturer of medical equipment in the United Kingdom, achieved registration using 32 procedures to describe its processes. An affiliated company, a small injection molding manufacturer in the U.S., borrowed the procedures and tried to customize them to fit its operation.

The injection molding company hired us to provide internal auditor training, and when we visited the company, we realized the problem at once. We helped redefine the processes, which eliminated twenty procedures, and the result was an appropriate, well-documented quality system.

Each organization is unique. Its quality system is unique, and its documentation must be as well. You may try to compete using someone else's system, but if your competitors are getting registered with their own systems, you will be at a decided disadvantage.

Implementing the Standard

"Implementing the Standard" is more common but just as troubling as "Implementing Someone Else's System." While this route can achieve registration, it saddles you with a system that is hard to understand and even harder to use, maintain, and audit.

With this approach, a procedure is written for each clause of the Standard rather than for the processes used by the company. Procedure titles are typically the same as the titles of the clauses in the Standard. "Contract review," "Document and data control," and "Inspection and testing" are examples. The activities that relate to a clause are documented in the respective procedures. There is no attempt to develop a flow or prevent overlap and duplication.

A team often determines how the organization meets each of the clauses. For example, the team for "product identification and traceability" determines where this requirement applies throughout the company. Each team writes a procedure for each of the clauses.

Such an approach creates procedures having major problems. The procedures are without substance, essentially converting the "you shalls" of the Standard into "we dos." The procedures only include those aspects that relate to the clause being addressed and are not logical, meaningful descriptions of the organization's processes. These flawed procedures have redundancies throughout and do not describe in a meaningful way how to operate the business.

The result is a set of procedures that has little relevance to the operation of the business and provides no guidance to employees. It can, however, fulfill the requirement allowing the company to become registered.

Summary

Beware if anyone tells you that your quality system will:
- have the same number of procedures as sections of the Standard,

- have more than 30 or less than 15 level-two procedures,
- require writing many new work instructions,
- require rewriting existing instructions, or
- have a quality manual of more than 30 pages. (Even registrars don't want to read voluminous quality manuals.)

A business meets its objectives through a series of interrelated processes, each with a defined purpose. Together, the processes allow the business to meet its overall objectives. The management of the processes is the management of the business, and "procedures" must describe these processes if they are to help in the management of the business.

Objectives

Like any successful project, the ISO 9000 registration effort needs clearly defined, realistic targets, or objectives. The first objective is a *realistic* target registration date, which for most organizations, is seven to fourteen months after the project is initiated.

Some managers say they are "working toward registration but haven't set a target date." Others say their objective is to be registered "in two years." It should not take that long. Projects that are extended over a long time tend to lose momentum and continuity. Registration projects that require some *stretch* and are not interrupted get better results and produce better quality systems.

Other Objectives

It is said that you only get out of something what you put into it. This is surely true for ISO 9000 registration. If management feels forced into registration by the market or considers registration to be an unreasonable, externally-imposed requirement, it has a "just-get-the-damn-thing-done" project. If management signs off and leaves the project to, say, the quality department, it has a low-priority project. On the other hand, if management views ISO 9000 registration as a strategic initiative, it has a meaningful project with sufficient attention and resources. Only then will ISO 9000 be strategic to the business and its market position.

Becoming registered to ISO 9000 means making changes. This need to change must be viewed as an opportunity to develop a sound quality system that will optimize work and increase control. If management has that attitude, the benefits will be far greater than an ISO 9000 certificate hanging on the wall.

> *Right now we are working with companies that don't care about earning the certificate. They have chosen to implement ISO 9000-compliant quality systems without going for registration. They just want the operating benefits that come from the required analysis, documentation, standardization, consistency, and control.*

High aspirations should be part of your program right from the beginning. At the outset, you must set objectives for productivity gains, increased customer satisfaction, and increased sales. TQM can be an objective. So can the other benefits discussed in Chapter Three. Turn your aspirations into business objectives, and develop strategies to achieve them.

Outside Assistance

Preparing an organization for ISO 9000 registration is not a small task. Even organizations planning to "do it themselves" can use some outside help in designing and documenting their quality systems. Written material, training programs, and consultants can all be useful resources.

Reading

The International Organization for Standardization publishes guidelines to help organizations apply the assessment standards to their particular businesses. See Figure 2.3 on page 16 for the four business types. While these guidelines are not required reading, they provide insight as to what a quality system should cover. A word of caution, however. The guidelines can cause the unwary to mistakenly believe that the requirements of the Standards are broader and more prescriptive than they actually are. Organizations will be registered to one of the assessment standards—not to a guideline.

If you are a do-it-yourself type, we recommend you acquire a how-to book that reflects the philosophy and approach you wish to adopt. Even if you plan to rely on an outside consultant, the book can help you choose the right consultant and help you manage the project.

Training

General ISO 9000

Introductory seminars can last a few hours or an entire day. The curriculum is similar to the contents of early chapters in this book, answering questions such as, "What is ISO 9000? What does registration involve? How long does registration take? How much does it cost? and Why are organizations getting registered?" If you attend a seminar and study the handout material, you should have enough background and understanding of ISO 9000 to make a well-informed decision about seeking registration.

Achieving ISO 9000 Registration

There are a number of public seminars, lasting from two to five days, that explain the requirements of the Standard and the necessary steps for registration—planning, documenting, and implementing a quality system. If one or two project leaders need to be trained, a public seminar makes sense. If you want to train the entire implementation team, on-site seminars are more cost-effective.

You need an experienced and reputable provider for training. Before choosing, ask several to explain their approach and strategy for registration; ask about their experience in helping other companies achieve registration. Book knowledge alone, or one-organization knowledge, is not adequate assurance that the provider knows the optimum approach or can accurately answer all questions.

Some organizations send their employees to different seminars. This sounds good in theory, but it doesn't work. There are several routes to ISO 9000 registration, and people tend to become "married" to the approach they learned in class. Such a team spends too much time arguing about which way to proceed.

Internal Auditor Training

The Standard requires internal audits to verify that the quality system is being used. This is an ongoing activity, second only to the initial documentation effort in the amount of resources required. It is important that the internal auditing program be well-planned. One or two project leaders should be trained to set up an effective internal auditing program. A two-day course should be sufficient. Strategies for effective internal auditing are discussed later.

Internal auditors also need training. Because a cross-section of employees should be on the team, it is usually most economical to have the internal auditors trained on-site. We train internal auditors in one or two days, but some courses last up to five days. The course should provide practice opportunities to reinforce learning and reference material for review prior to subsequent audits.

Internal auditors don't have to know the details of the ISO 9000 Standard. Their job is to verify the use of the quality system—not compliance to the Standard. See Figure 4.5 on page 78. Compliance to the Standard is designed into the quality system.

Lead Auditor Training

Many larger organizations send project leaders and others who deal with the registrar to lead auditor training. These classes satisfy the first requirement for becoming a lead auditor, but they do not offer instruction on how to get registered. Instead, course participants learn how registrars and auditors think and operate—which can be useful in anticipating the audit and relating to the auditors.

A quality manager who worked for an automobile manufacturer attended one of the earlier lead auditor courses. After he completed the course, his boss asked if he could plan and carry out what the company needed to do to become registered. He responded, "No, but I can tell you if you're doing it wrong!"

Lead auditor courses are designed to equip registrar auditors with the skills and knowledge they need to verify that a quality system meets the requirements of the Standard. This is not the same kind of knowledge required for designing a system that meets the Standard's requirements.

At competitive swim meets, officials watch for illegal strokes, false starts, and other penalties that disqualify a swimmer. The training and skills an official needs are very different from a coach's, whose job is to teach the swimmers stroke techniques and race strategies and train them for stamina and speed.

Consulting Assistance

Organizations that need more than outside training can hire a consultant to help them through the project. When a consultant is used, it is most important to choose one with the right experience and a successful ISO 9000 track record. Again, choose someone who has helped more than just a few companies achieve registration.

There is more involved here than just registration. The consultant needs to have a broad knowledge of systems and management control. Building an optimum quality system requires knowledge of such management issues as organization theory, process management, delegation, staff appraisal, and contract law. A keen understanding of quality issues such as product liability, reliability, and process control is also necessary.

> *We know of a company that hired a consultant who had experience with only two other quality systems. The company wasted three years and $50,000 developing an inappropriate system which was later discarded.*

Organizations usually need the most help during the documentation phase, and they can choose between two approaches.

With the first approach, the consultant provides training, reviews the system when documented, answers questions, and gives advice. The consultant's first task is to understand the business: its way of operating and its resources. The next step is to set up a training program to teach the client team how to document an effective quality system. The consultant then monitors the documentation as it is prepared by the team.

The other approach is for the consultant to lead the documentation effort. This may be the only option for smaller organizations. We have taken this approach for more than 150 clients. All were registered following their first audit—and without pre-assessment.

We start with a client's current way of operating and make changes that improve the business and ensure compliance to the Standard. The result is always the same—*the client's quality system*. This method is the fastest and surest way to a documented quality system. The "document-it-yourself" learning curve is overcome by an experienced quality consultant—and the client ends up with an effective quality system and prompt registration.

The consultant's role in the implementation/operation phase should not be major. Only the organization can operate its system. Internal auditors must be trained, and this is best done by a consultant using a developed and tested course. Consultants can provide advice and suggestions throughout the operating phase. Even if the consultant is heavily involved, one or more of the organization's employees must be well versed in the quality system and ISO 9000. This is essential for the ongoing viability of the quality system.

Choosing a Consultant

When choosing among consultants, the two most important factors to consider are their approaches to registration and their relevant experience with the Standard. How do they approach the documentation requirement? By documenting to the Standard? How many times have they been through the entire registration process? *One time—a sample size of one—is not enough.* Too many organizations have used consultants lacking the proper knowledge or experience. While attaining registration, many have ended up with inefficient, bureaucratic systems. That is not the type of experience you want to hire.

> *At a meeting of consultants the attendees were asked to introduce themselves. One proudly said that he had been working in the field of ISO 9000 for over 2 years; his first client was being assessed next month. Is that the experience you want to buy?*

Hire someone with registration experience, whose approach corresponds to yours, who agrees with you on the type of system you need, and who believes there is more to ISO 9000 than the certificate. Hire someone you are comfortable with; a firm that is itself registered to ISO 9000—one that "practices what it preaches."

Organizing and Assigning the Resources

Whether or not you are working with a consultant, you will still need some project organization and a project team. A typical project organization is shown in Figure 4.3.

Management Representative for Quality

The Standard requires that executive management identify a member of management as the Management Representative for Quality. This is not a full-time job, and being a "quality specialist" is not a prerequisite. Most important, the designated executive or

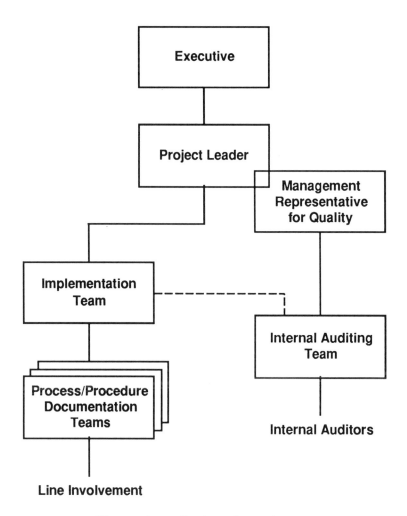

Figure 4.3   Project Organization

manager must have the desire to champion the cause of quality and ensure an effective quality system.

Many companies have a quality manager in place before making the commitment to seek ISO 9000 registration. They need to decide whether this individual should become the "Management Representative for Quality." If the quality specialist is not already part of management, we do not advise promotion just for the sake of ISO 9000. However, if executive management wants the quality specialist to be part of management for all issues, the promotion would signal a commitment to quality.

The position of Management Representative for Quality does not have to be filled by a manager from the quality department. In many small organizations the role is taken by the chief executive or plant manager. Other small companies choose the financial controller or the head of design, sales, or operations. Because the quality system involves the entire organization, quality is everybody's business, and every manager is a potential candidate. It is more important to choose the right person than to select someone because of rank or position.

The Management Representative does not have to personally perform all the activities required by the position but must be the focal point that ensures the quality system is effective. The work can be shared by the entire organization, and much of the administrative work can be delegated.

Project Leader

The Project Leader has the responsibility to get the organization registered. The senior executive, especially in a smaller organization, could very well assume this role. Other candidates for Project Leader could be a senior manager from operations or quality or another staff person who is good at managing such projects.

The preferred candidate for project leader is the Management Representative for Quality. This individual has the ongoing responsibility for quality as well as a vested interest in the smooth implementation and effective quality system. The Project Leader and Management Representative for Quality positions can be filled by two people, but there are obvious advantages if one person assumes both roles.

The Project Leader's main responsibilities are:

- choosing the implementation team,
- obtaining the required training and outside assistance, and
- managing the project to successful registration.

Implementation Team

The implementation team should represent all impacted areas of the organization. If registration to ISO 9001 is the objective, someone from product development should be included. The team should develop an implementation plan and is responsible for the successful completion of the project. Team members should take the lead in documenting and implementing the quality system in their particular areas. When all areas and functions are involved, the likelihood increases that the system will be accepted.

The Implementation Team

Charter
- Achieve ISO 9000 registration

Membership
- 4 to 8 members
- Managers and professionals
- Representation from entire organization
- Management Representative for Quality

Training
- ISO 9000 Standard requirements
- ISO 9000 documentation requirements
- Defining/designing processes
- Documenting processes

Leader
- Management Representative for Quality preferred, but more important, someone who commands respect and can lead a major project.

Process/Procedure Documentation Team and Line Involvement

The quality system should not be documented without input from those who do the work. Area personnel know how the work is now done, and the implementation team member knows what the Standard requires. Working together, they can document procedures and work instructions that everyone understands and wants to use. Documentation teams, if formally established, should be organized as shown in the box.

Process/Procedure Documentation Team

Charter
  • Write ISO 9000-compliant procedures and work instructions
  • Finalize and implement these procedures and work instructions

Membership
  • Someone from implementation team
  • Employees with knowledge of the processes being documented
  • Optionally, an independent "analyst"

Training
  • Organization's format for documenting procedures and work instructions
  • Overview of ISO 9000 requirements applicable to particular area

Leader
  • Implementation team member

There are benefits in having an independent "analyst" examine, question, and suggest changes to processes before they are documented. This is true whether the analyst is a trained colleague or an external consultant.

The quality system should be implemented as each document is completed. This is much less disruptive than installing all procedures and work instructions at the same time. When line employees are involved in the documentation, they have fewer problems implementing the system. Remember: *a compliant system that is operated as documented achieves registration.*

Internal Audit Team

Internal auditing is a never-ending requirement of the Standard. The internal audit team is responsible for these audits and should include executives, managers, professional staff, and even hourly employees. Team members can be from all functional areas, including those not under the ISO 9000 scope, such as accounting.

Internal auditing is an important activity that can help the organization continually improve its quality system and operation. It starts when operation of the documented quality system begins. It continues for as long as the organization is registered.

Internal Audit Team

Charter
- Carry out internal audits and report findings

Membership
- All levels of the organization including executives and Chief Executive
- All functions of the organization
- Enough so that team members do one to three audits per quarter

Training
- General requirements of ISO 9000
- Planning and conducting audits and reporting the findings

Leader
- Management Representative for Quality

Summary

These organizational structures are for all organizations. Those with fewer employees will have smaller teams. Figure 4.4 on page 76 shows that the ISO 9000 registration effort requires the involvement of all of management and most employees.

Internal Auditing

Internal auditing is vital to the successful operation of the quality system and the eventual return on investment from ISO

9000. After the documentation of the quality system, internal auditing is the most resource-consuming activity in achieving and maintaining registration. The Standard requires that organizations periodically perform audits to verify that "planned arrangements" are being followed. The Standard does not specify how the requirement is to be satisfied. There are two main issues and decisions—scheduling the audits and deciding who does them.

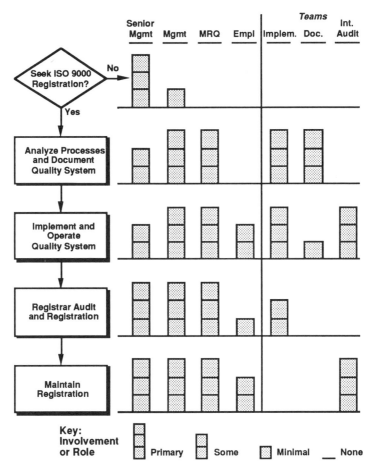

Figure 4.4   Model for Involvement

Audits are best scheduled by procedure and/or groups of procedures. Since the procedures reflect all of the Standard's requirements, auditing them is auditing the Standard's requirements. Auditing by procedure is more meaningful and generates more improvements than auditing against the Standard.

Some organize their internal audits by clause of the Standard. For example, one audit is scheduled to address "Inspection and Test Status" throughout the system. Although accepted by registrars, audits conducted in this manner are more time-consuming and difficult to conduct than audits by procedure. To audit against the Standard, internal auditors must understand and be able to interpret all elements of the Standard.

While it may sound appealing to assign one or two auditors to do all the audits, it seldom works. Because internal auditing is a routine job and a dead-end assignment, even dedicated auditors lose their effectiveness over time.

Outsiders—either consultants or staff from another facility—have been used for internal audits. This is contrary to the spirit of the Standard and not conducive to maintaining a culture of self-improvement in the organization.

The internal audit team should be a cross section of employees by rank and function and include executives, managers, technical and professional employees, and other employees. Ideally, the top executive of the unit being registered is on the team.

Functions such as accounting, although not in the scope of ISO 9000 should be represented. Internal auditors do not have to be experts in the Standard. Their job is to verify the use of the quality system (see Figure 4.5). Using such a diverse group for internal auditing is an approach that not only works but produces extra benefits as well. It gives more and different employees the opportunity to get involved. It is also a good cross-training opportunity and provides fresh "eyes" for audits.

Figure 4.5   Internal Auditing

One Saturday we conducted an internal auditor training seminar for a chemical company. The plant manager, production employees, and others were in the class. The following Monday the plant manager called and happily exclaimed that including two production workers on the audit team was a great decision. As he walked through the plant Monday morning, employees let him know they understood the importance of complying with the system and were anticipating what ISO 9000 could do for the company. The plant manager had made the right decision to include production people and had chosen the right ones to participate.

Internal audits should be taken seriously. They are part of the mechanism to improve the business, as shown in Figure 2.5 on page 22. Choose a broad-based team, and give team members good training. Then follow through on their findings. Internal audits produce process improvements.

Selecting and Hiring a Registrar

You must hire a registrar to audit and register the organization to ISO 9000. Make sure you choose the right one—the relationship is generally long-term. Fortunately there are many registrars from which to choose. In the United Kingdom, there are over 30 organizations accredited to conduct audits and grant ISO 9000 registration. In North America, there are close to fifty. Be sure to consider the following criteria when making your choice:

- accreditation,
- expertise and experience,
- mode of operation,
- cost, and
- availability.

Accreditation

Be sure the registrar you select is accredited by a recognized national accreditation body. Your audits and registration will be conducted under the rules and requirements of that body. See Figure 2.2 on page 15. Some registrars, usually the ones advertising low audit fees, are not accredited.

Accredited registrars operate in accordance with ISO Standard 10011, Guidelines for Auditing Quality Systems. Like ISO-registered companies, they are free to operate however they want—as long as their operating systems and practices satisfy the Standard.

Accrediting bodies are national, but not all countries have them. Currently, three major accrediting bodies account for most of the registrations being done today. They are:

- National Accreditation Council
  for Certification Bodies (NACCB)   United Kingdom
- Raad Voor de Certificatie (RVC)   Netherlands
- Registrar Accreditation Board (RAB)   United States

Registrars are accredited by one or more national accrediting bodies. The larger ones are often accredited by all three of those mentioned, and others as well. Multiple accreditations enable registrars to register organizations under any or all national designations.

Each accreditation body has slightly different requirements, evaluation schemes, and operating rules. The goal of ISO 9000 is to have common requirements for all accrediting bodies and registrars.

You must determine if the registrar and accreditation body are important to your current and future customers and market. Another consideration may be your product. If the product is regulated in Europe, it may need a *CE* mark to be sold. It could be advantageous to choose a registrar that is also a notified body for *CE* product certification. This would allow some organization to conduct both the ISO 9000 registration and *CE* mark audits.

Expertise and Experience

In order to be accredited in an industry, a registrar must perform successful audits in that industry under the observation of the accrediting body. Some registrars specialize in specific industries; others prefer a wider scope. It is important that your registrar have experience and expertise in your particular type of business. Such a registrar would be likely to understand the processes and controls you use. Equally important is hiring a firm that has audited organizations the size of yours and is comfortable doing so.

Mode of Operation

Registrars have different ways of operating, particularly with regard to pre-audit contacts, evaluation approaches, post-audit surveillances, and re-registration.

Some registrars send a salesperson to estimate the cost of the audit, but provide no information about it. Others request a chargeable pre-audit visit to meet with your staff, learn about your operation, and review documentation for possible deficiencies. A third approach, common in North America, is a desk review, where the organization submits its quality manual to the registrar for review. This approach provides definitive feedback and saves money if the registrar is not local. But without a visit, it is hard for the registrar to determine if the documented system relates to the operation, and it is hard for you to establish a relationship with your registrar.

There are two ways a registrar evaluates the results of an audit. In both, your quality system and operation are evaluated against each element of the Standard. The first method determines whether your organization satisfies all the applicable elements with no major deficiency in any element. If so, the registrar recommends registration upon correction of minor noncompliances.

In the other, your system and operation are evaluated against each element and given a score. To achieve registration, you must have an average score of 75 percent or better, with no element scoring lower than 65 percent. If you fail, you know immediately the areas that need to be corrected. The fee for these audits is higher.

Either way, you will have to correct all noncompliances before registration is granted, and you are usually given three months to do so. Depending on the corrective actions required, you may need another on-site audit. Or it may be enough to send evidentiary documentation to the registrar to ensure the "pass" recommendation.

Once your company is registered, the registrar will most likely conduct two surveillance visits a year, depending on how well your company performed in the initial and subsequent audits. The surveillance visits are not as long or detailed as the initial audit. If noncompliances are found during a surveillance audit, you will have to respond. If they are not major, they will be checked at the next surveillance visit. Major noncompliances require extra visits, and if corrective action is not taken, registration will be withdrawn.

Registration certificates are either open-ended or are issued for a fixed amount of time, usually three or four years. Open-ended registration is maintained solely by surveillance audits. When a fixed-time certificate expires, another full assessment is conducted and a new certificate issued. This re-assessment is more extensive than a surveillance audit and is similar to the initial registration audit.

Cost

Registrars usually charge a registration fee, a daily fee for auditor time, and billable expenses. Travel cost, usually the largest billable expense, can be reduced by selecting a registrar with local auditors. When you compare costs, we recommend that you calculate them for the first five years to cover variations in the different operating policies. Registrar fees are discussed in Chapter 2.

Availability

Be sure to start early in your search for a registrar. Begin when the registration process begins, especially if you have a tight time line. By starting early, you should be able to hire the registrar you want and schedule the audit for when you want it.

First, call a number of registrars and ask each to send you an application and literature. Complete and return the application to receive a quote. Four to six proposals should be plenty for you to choose from. The registrar's responses and any conversations or visits should give you ample information to make a good choice.

Pre-Assessment Audit

Your organization will need a readiness check prior to the registrar's audit. This check can be done by your own people or by an outsider. You don't need to decide who you want for the job until after your quality system is in operation. If the system is running smoothly, you may decide you don't need an outside evaluation and instead use your own staff.

There is no requirement that says you have to hire your registrar, or anyone else, to do a readiness check. But many organizations, particularly those lacking ISO 9000 experience, want a pre-assessment. Some even believe it is necessary. Our clients have been registered on the first audit without pre-assessment.

Opting for a pre-assessment does not guarantee registration. Only part of the quality system is tested in any audit. Noncompliances, even major ones, can be missed. Furthermore, a registrar's interpretations and evaluations will not always be the same tomorrow as they are today. Something that looked fine in pre-assessment might not look so good during the subsequent audit.

And pre-assessments don't count. A registrar's audit is required for *every* organization going through the ISO 9000 registration process—even the one that breezed through its pre-assessment with only a handful of minor noncompliances.

> *One company's registrar spent the same number of auditor days for the pre-assessment as it did for the registration audit itself. The company easily passed the pre-assessment with a score of over 90 percent. Two months later, it did not pass the final audit. Why? The employees were so pleased with their pre-assessment score that they became complacent. They neither completed internal audits as scheduled nor followed up on corrective actions— major breaches of the internal auditing requirement.*

Getting registered without a pre-assessment almost always costs less than registration with one. Even in the worst case (not passing the audit), it is no more expensive. An organization with major noncompliances requiring a complete re-audit will pay about the same as for a pre-assessment and registration audit.

If you build and implement a sound quality system, you will achieve ISO 9000 registration—with or without pre-assessment. Every organization has some noncompliances and is given time to correct them before being recommended for registration.

If our arguments haven't convinced you to skip the pre-assessment, your next step is to find someone to conduct it. You could use a trained employee from your organization. We don't recommend using a volunteer who is looking for auditing experience. We believe that your best bet is to hire your registrar or an experienced consultant. Your pre-assessment should be scheduled from eight to twelve weeks before the registration audit. This will give you ample time to correct noncompliances.

Summary

Whether your goal is a registration certificate, or registration with a quality system that adds value to the organization, you need to make some important decisions before and during the implementation of your quality system.

This chapter identified the issues and choices along with our recommendations. We trust you can now make the right decisions for your organization.

Even in these times of self-directed work teams and empowerment, management leadership is still needed. This is certainly true in the pursuit of ISO 9000 registration.

Chapter Four discussed the decisions management must make to ensure an efficient registration and further benefits. *This chapter defines management's leadership and role* both while pursuing registration and after registration is attained. Both management and the implementers have key roles in achieving registration, but it is management's role that ensures additional benefits from the ISO 9000 investment.

Chapter 5

Management's Role

In This Chapter:

- Leading the effort to get registered
- Keeping the effort on track
- Developing a quality policy
- Communicating to the organization
- Chairing management reviews
- Participating in internal audits
- Impacting functional areas

Many organizations are either already pursuing ISO 9000 registration or preparing to do so. Yours may be one of them. Our earlier chapters discussed and answered questions about ISO 9000 and the registration process. To give our readers an edge, we delved also into the aspects of ISO 9000 that most executives do not consider. We emphasized the importance of management's attention to ensure an efficient registration and a value-adding system. We wanted you to be informed and confident you were making the right choices regarding ISO 9000.

Now you have chosen ISO 9000. Your desired outcome should be more than the registration certificate. You want a system that adds value and improves the business. Registration is not the "end" but the "means" to something more.

Leadership

Executive management needs to set high expectations and see that those expectations are achieved. Managers must support the effort by actions as well as words. They need to be visible and involved. To use a common expression, they need to "walk the talk."

Executive management must lead the ISO 9000 registration effort. But obviously, executives cannot validate every decision so they must delegate. Delegation does not negate the need for leadership and involvement. Instead of saying, "I am committed to this goal," executives must assert, "You can count on my involvement until our goal is realized."

Leadership is structured involvement, not random interference. When management is involved in the quality system, it communicates their commitment to the entire organization. *If management does not make that commitment, no one else does either.* By having the quality system routinely audited by outside experts, the chief executive demonstrates a strong commitment to quality.

The ISO 9000 registration process requires executive involvement, and the executives in our client companies have told us it is time well spent. Many chief executives have been surprised by how much they learned about their own firms while members of their ISO 9000 teams. By taking part in the design, implementation, assessment, and maintenance of processes, they learn how their organizations operate. They also learn how quality is perceived by their suppliers, customers, and employees. They have found the experience most worthwhile.

It is not our purpose to talk about being a leader. No doubt, you already are one. Our point is that ISO 9000 is important and must be in executive management's sphere. You must be interested, engaged, involved, and in the lead. The next sections discuss the scope of that involvement.

Develop Quality Policy and Objectives

Section 4.1.1 of ISO 9001, 9002, and 9003 says:

> "...management with executive responsibility shall define and document its policy for quality, including objectives for quality and its commitment to quality. The quality policy shall be relevant to the supplier's organizational goals and the expectations and needs of its customers. The supplier shall ensure that this policy is understood, implemented, and maintained at all levels of the organization."

It is important to develop a quality policy and quality objectives that reflect the thinking of executive management and the entire management team. It should be a policy that everyone believes in, that everyone owns, and to which everyone feels committed.

Executive management must take whatever time is needed to develop a quality policy and objectives. They need to focus on the role quality plays in the company and their level of commitment to it. Then other managers and even employees need to discuss the concept of quality and what it means in the company.

Developing a quality policy is far more beneficial than adopting someone else's policy or asking the Management Representative or a consultant to write a policy. That would be a meaningless exercise, even though it might appear to save time and effort at the beginning.

The policy should not be a "feel good" statement, nor should it be an adaptation of nice-sounding words that merely satisfy the Standard's requirements.

The time set apart for the development of this policy can be a time of growth for the management team, and the process itself as useful as the outcome. It gives all team members the opportunity to state and discuss their beliefs and come to a consensus concerning quality, what the company stands for, and what its relationships with customers really mean.

The outcome, of course, is critical. It is a public statement of management's beliefs and leadership. Once the policy is made public, commitment to it is essential. A wise manager doesn't write "We always put quality first," and then tell an employee that a faulty item is good enough to ship. The quality policy is the target *of* and *for* management. If it is not followed, the employees are the first to know. For quality to succeed, leadership is essential.

The Standard does not specify the content or length of the quality policy. It may be several paragraphs or a list of statements. The quality policy should address the organization's intentions, vision and direction, objectives, commitment, and customers.

Intentions

What does the organization intend to do about quality? Is it prepared to allocate the necessary resources? This is the place to define quality, as understood by the organization in its environment.

Vision and Direction

Where is the organization going? Is it content with present quality, or does it believe in continual improvement? Is there a vision and direction for quality? The answers could determine the future of the organization.

Objectives

The overall goal for quality needs to be clearly defined within the corporate policy, including an indication of strategy to be taken.

Commitment

An organization's commitment to quality may be expressed in statements such as, "Quality is our first priority at all times." Does this mean "quality at any price"? No. Gold plating may provide the highest level of protection against corrosion, but if the customers' needs can be met using zinc, then zinc plating would be "the appropriate quality" in that circumstance.

Customers

To be meaningful and relevant, a quality policy must address the needs and expectations of the customer. How these are determined is just as important as how they are achieved. Are they set by the customer or developed and influenced by the organization? Expectations constantly change. Does the organization plan to meet them, or does it want to exceed them?

The Quality Policy

The quality policy must be clear and understandable even if all of the above considerations are not addressed. It must be meaningful to all concerned and it must be truthful. The quality policy is the standard by which management can judge the performance of the organization. It is also the standard by which the organization can—and will—judge management.

The quality policy must appear in the quality manual and be prominently displayed. All employees should have access to copies of the policy, and they should understand how it applies to them. A good way to accomplish this awareness training is from the top down, with managers training their own people. Then employees in each section of the organization can be shown how the policy applies to them.

Management's Roles

Management's involvement is required in both the registration project and the subsequent operation of the quality system. After all, a quality system is about identifying and satisfying the needs of customers. It defines how the business is operated so customers are satisfied and keep coming back. After initiating the registration effort, executive management has four additional major roles:

- management of the project,
- communication to employees,
- management review, and
- internal auditing.

Management of the Project

No matter how plentiful the internal resources or how extensive the outside assistance, management must still organize and lead the registration effort. It is management's responsibility to effect the efficient registration of a quality system. To oversee the ISO 9000 registration project, management needs to empower an implementation team and hold it accountable.

An important rule for SCUBA divers is, "Plan the dive, then dive the plan." The same principle applies here. Once an implementation plan is developed, it must be used or it loses its value. Plans change, but the plan enables the effects of changes to be determined.

The plan supports the progress of the project, and when the plan is used, timely compliance is more likely. For the plan to have any value, everyone must understand it, accept it, be committed to it, and believe it is achievable.

The progress of the registration project can be easily monitored if the plan has frequent, identifiable milestones. The implementation team controls the day-to-day activities of the project, and executive management reviews progress at least monthly. Where the milestones are not being achieved, management needs to act. The objective is not so much to place blame, but to find out how to bring the project back into line.

Few management participants want to discuss the details of every process and procedure; it is not an effective use of their time. Instead, project review meetings are held for general issues—those impacting several organization functions. The development of a training strategy, a company-wide activity, is an example of a general issue. Project review meetings involving the implementation team and executive management are an ideal lead-in for the ISO 9000-required management reviews that will follow.

The organization's registration plan should be published, and all employees should know key target dates such as the start of internal audits, the registrar's initial visit, pre-assessment, etc. Milestones that are reached, achievements, significant progress—all should be reported. Quality is everyone's business, and everyone should know what's happening.

Quality is a team game, and management should be there to provide support for the team. The game has one objective—to meet or surpass the needs and expectations of customers. This doesn't happen by accident but only when there is a game plan that everyone understands and supports. A plan supported with resources, skills, commitment, and knowledge practically guarantees success.

Communication to Employees

ISO 9000 may be one of the largest and most visible projects an organization will undertake. Many employees are involved in designing and documenting the quality system, and all will use it. Employee interest and need for information are high. Figure 5.1 identifies four points, each at the beginning of a new phase, where formal communication to employees is needed. The communication should convey, "Here's where we've been," and "This is what's next." Where practical, these communications should be conveyed by the chief executive. How you choose to have the information presented depends on what works best in your organization.

1. Decision to Seek Registration

Once you make the decision to seek registration to ISO 9000, tell all your employees. Your communication should include:

- what ISO 9000 is,
- what ISO 9000 registration is,
- why ISO 9000 is important to the organization,
- what is involved in becoming registered,
- who will be involved in the registration process,
- how ISO 9000 will impact and change people's jobs and the operation of the business, and
- the timetable for the project.

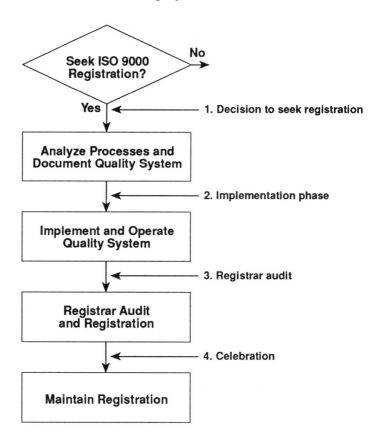

Figure 5.1 Model for Communication

2. Operation Phase

During the documentation phase, processes are analyzed and the quality system is documented. When most of the documentation has been completed, you are ready to implement and operate the quality system, *i.e.,* operate the business as documented. Everyone whose job impacts quality is now involved, and internal audits are about to begin. Your communication needs to address:

- the organization's quality policy and objectives,
- the status of the documentation phase,
- the output of the documentation phase—quality manual, procedures, and work instructions,
- what is involved in operating the system (*i.e.,* using it as documented, document control, internal audits, corrective action),
- what internal audits are and why they are necessary,
- who the internal auditors are, and
- why it is important to conduct the work as documented.

3. Registrar Audit

Prior to the registrar audit, you should communicate with employees, giving them guidance and reassurance, including:

- the auditors' plan and schedule,
- how auditors operate,
- who the auditors might talk to and what they might ask,
- how to respond if questioned, and
- to learn the quality policy and objectives.

Remind employees that the most knowledgeable people will be with the auditors at all times. If other employees are questioned, they should answer honestly and to the best of their ability. While they need to understand the quality policy and objectives well enough to explain it in their own words, memorization is not necessary.

4. Celebration

Before they leave, the auditors will tell you if you will be registered without another visit. We consider that to be a "pass." If you passed, celebrate! You are essentially registered. Your certificate will be issued once minor noncompliances are corrected. Good news travels fast—your employees will already know, but take the time to do the following things.

- Congratulate everyone. ISO 9000 registration is truly a major accomplishment.
- Thank everyone. It was a team effort, and everyone helped.
- Explain the auditors' report, including what still must be done.
- Remind employees that registration is a beginning and not an end. Everyone must continue to use and improve the system and the business.

Management Review

Section 4.1.3 of ISO 9000 reads:

> "The supplier's management with executive responsibility shall review the quality system at defined intervals sufficient to ensure its continuing suitability and effectiveness in satisfying the requirements of this International Standard and the supplier's stated quality policy and objectives. Records of such reviews shall be maintained."

The Standard requires that management review the operation of the quality system. It does not specify what the reviews should include or how often they should be held. Management makes those decisions. It is best to begin management reviews shortly after beginning the implementation and operation of the quality system.

The reviews should be attended by all executives, non-management specialists, and initially, at least, any outside consultant. During the management review meetings held prior to registration, managers may report on progress in their areas of responsibility, share common problems, and develop solutions. They identify required actions, assign responsibility, and allocate resources. Because of the holistic nature of a business, its quality system is enhanced when all executives are involved in management reviews.

An organization identifies, defines, and meets its customers' requirements with many processes. The management of these processes should ensure the necessary level of quality. Because processes usually involve several different functions of the organization, optimization is achieved when all functions are subordinated to the total system. Once the quality system is up and operating, management reviews should cover:

- problems and issues,
- the results of internal audits,
- customer return and complaint data,
- other quality results and measures,
- supplier concerns,
- corrective actions from earlier meetings,
- training assessments and plans,
- communications and issues concerning the ISO 9000 registration, and
- changes that impact the quality system.

The management review team chooses how to evaluate and use the internal audit results. Some organizations summarize the audits, while others study each audit report in detail and discuss auditors' findings. Either way is acceptable. The internal audit review must cover, at minimum, auditors' findings and the effectiveness of corrective and preventive actions.

Management also needs to review problem and noncompliance data. These data typically include customer complaints, returns, warranty repairs, internal rejects, and supplier concerns. Again, every item need not be considered in detail, but evidence should be provided that an appropriate review was conducted in each case. The real evidence of effectiveness comes when noncompliances disappear altogether.

Management also needs to review communications from the registrar and appropriate follow-up actions. Registrar communications include the results of surveillance visits, details of future visits, changes in the registrar's procedures, and information on any forthcoming changes to the Standard.

When an organization's activities are governed or affected by legislation and/or regulations, the impact of these changes must be determined. Such changes may have no direct impact, or they may have far-reaching effects. Either way, they should be discussed at review meetings.

Changes in the business such as new products, processes, services, facilities, and methods will affect the quality system. These changes need to be addressed proactively and plans reviewed by management. Such changes frequently lead to equipment additions and personnel changes. If that is the case, training plans will probably need to be updated.

Combining management reviews with other meetings is not a good idea. The presence of other issues could lessen the necessary focus on the quality system. Management reviews work when they are held before or after other meetings, but separate from them. An organization's regular "quality" meetings can evolve into management review meetings, although their scope will probably have to be broadened in order to fully meet the requirements of the Standard.

The Standard does not specify what the frequency of management reviews must be. Some registered organizations only have annual reviews. We question whether such infrequent reviews can provide full value—and value is important.

During the initial stages of the registration process, a monthly review is almost essential. A month is long enough for planned activities to be completed and short enough for feedback to be timely and, therefore, effective. Once registration is achieved, the frequency of management reviews can be adjusted. But if the time between reviews is longer than two months, control and focus can be lost.

Management reviews are an essential part of the quality system and are clearly executive management's responsibility. They give management the opportunity to examine various elements of the system for effectiveness and suitability. When conducted in earnest, these reviews are vital to improving the business. They are also a means for executives to assure their organizations of the high priority they give to quality and their quality system.

Internal Auditing

In earlier chapters, we made the case for a broad-based internal audit team that included executive management and, preferably, the chief executive of the organization. The make-up of the audit team is crucial to its becoming a real, value-adding quality system. With executive management and other senior managers involved, internal auditing is given its proper standing. When internal auditing is left only to the quality department, without management involvement, it loses authority and is often ineffective.

Conducting audits demonstrates management's commitment to quality. Other employees realize the importance of quality when they see management's involvement.

There are other benefits as well. Executive managers have told us that when they do internal audits, they learn things about their organizations they couldn't have learned any other way. Once executives understand problems, the problems get fixed.

> *The CEO of a manufacturing company had to audit its pro-duction-planning process. He had no direct knowledge of, or prior experience in the area, but was convinced it was a bottleneck. He was looking forward to learning how the process worked.*
>
> *Although the audit took valuable time, it proved to be most fruitful and time well spent. The CEO learned there was a need for additional computer resources. New equipment was ordered with the full support of the auditor—the CEO.*

In some cases, including executives on the internal audit team creates problems. The word "audit" produces a negative response for many. Couple that feeling with the fact that executives will be doing some audits, and employees will often be apprehensive.

> *We once trained twenty internal auditors for a 400-employee manufacturer. The top executives were in the class, including the CEO, who was autocratic, loud, and demanding. Midway through the class, it was apparent that many employees were afraid of him and dreaded the thought of his auditing their departments.*

Employee apprehension is reduced when internal audits are communicated and positioned properly. It must be emphasized that the quality system is being audited, not individuals. The objective of internal auditing is to improve the operation of the business. Everyone must understand that intent. It is also important for managers to leave their "management hats" back in the office. When conducting internal audits, auditors, no matter what their rank or position, must only wear internal auditor hats. Conversely, when being audited, managers must respect the role of the auditor, regardless of position in the organization.

As illustrated in Figure 5.2, internal audits, management reviews, and corrective and preventive actions provide the mechanism to improve a business.

Functional Areas

ISO 9000 impacts all functional areas. Organizations will experience some changes in their operating practices. The extent of these changes depends on the current practices of the company. The main issues facing management are discussed following Figure 5.2.

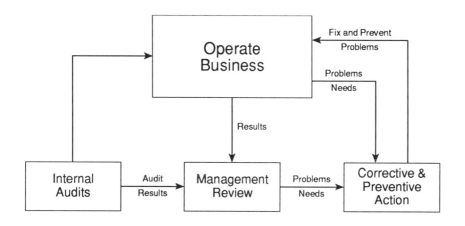

Figure 5.2   The ISO 9000 Systems Improvement Loop

Sales

When a company is registered to ISO 9000, its sales contracts must ensure that products and services are clearly defined and the sale is within the known capability of the company. Sales literature and advertising must not be misleading and should be reviewed for accuracy by the company's design or technical function. If such a review does not reveal any concerns, the sales department knows it

101

has an accurate understanding of how the product or service performs. When there are concerns, and there often are, they can be addressed, avoiding the chance of misrepresentation.

The terms and conditions of a sale must be specified. We have been amazed by the number of clients, particularly in service industries, whose contracts do not contain formal conditions. Formalized conditions are essential to avoid misunderstandings and to clarify what is expected from both the supplier and the customer.

Before an order is accepted, the capability and capacity aspects of the order need to be verified. The technical details are often included in sales literature, but for specialty products and services, a technical authority might be needed to review the quotation or order. If, at the time of quoting, there is any uncertainty concerning delivery time, there should be a caveat that delivery will be confirmed at the time of order. No one can be 100% certain that a delivery date will be met, but when the company makes a time commitment, it must be reasonably sure it can be honored. When delays are encountered, the customer needs to be informed.

Quality does not mean perfection, and there are times when the service or product falls below the needs and expectations of the customer—who may then complain. Complaints should be seen as opportunities for improvement. ISO 9000 requires that complaints and concerns be recorded, investigated, and the causes determined.

At least two actions are required after a customer complains. First, remedial action must be taken to satisfy that particular concern. The product may be replaced, money refunded, or the customer compensated, depending on the nature of the concern. If this is an isolated instance, further action may not be necessary. Otherwise, some corrective or preventive action is necessary. A clearer definition of the product may be all that is required. A complaint, even a serious one, when handled professionally, can result in improved customer relations and service.

Design

When a company designs its own products or services, those who are responsible for the design process must ensure that certain controls are exercised.

The design must start with a clear definition of what is required. This may be in the form of a design brief, a target specification, or a series of objectives. The definition needs to be formally recorded and agreed to by all parties associated with the design process.

The sales or marketing function, together with operations and purchasing, is also usually involved in the design definition and agreement process. Where a design is customer-specific, the customer should be involved as well. Everyone affected by the finished design should agree on the definition of the design output. With ISO 9000, the design function is not isolated.

Once there is agreement on the design, a plan needs to be drawn up, resources must be assigned, and milestones posted.

There must be periodic design reviews for all interested parties to confirm that the design objectives are being met. If the objectives are changed during a review, a formal recorded agreement is necessary. The process of review, change, and approval continues until there is consensus that the original design requirements, subject to agreed modifications, have been met.

Models, prototypes, or pilot runs may be needed to validate the design. The close cooperation and agreement of all involved parties ensures that the finished design will be acceptable to everyone.

A major responsibility of the design function is to maintain written records that define what is being done and why. This documentation may be in the form of drawings, instructions, recipes or specifications—all necessary to ensure that a design is carried out.

Purchasing

The method for approving suppliers and sub-contractors must be formalized prior to registration. Companies often have long-standing relationships with many of their suppliers. These suppliers can be approved on the basis of their past performance, and there is no need to assess them.

You must, however, be sure to provide evidence that a supplier has been officially approved. We recommend maintaining a record for each supplier, indicating past approval and the name of the person who authorized that approval. This is the simplest and best route to take. Further assessment of existing suppliers is not a requirement of the Standard and would only add cost without adding value.

Most organizations have an established routine for assessing new suppliers. Samples may be obtained, references requested, and the premises of the supplier may be visited. The Standard does not require a specific method of approval. If your assessment routine ensures the quality of the product or service, then it is acceptable. Just make sure there is evidence of the assessment and its results.

There are two common misconceptions about the Standard's purchasing requirements. The first is that registered companies can only buy from other registered companies. This is not a requirement, but a policy an organization may wish to adopt. The second misconception is that suppliers must complete a questionnaire before approval. Although it is a widespread practice, this is a waste of time and effort.

Once a supplier or sub-contractor is approved, its performance needs to be continually monitored and its status periodically reviewed. No company should ignore a supplier that sends bad material. For an effective supplier-management system, each instance of a supplier sending unacceptable goods must be recorded, along with the action taken.

All contracts with suppliers and sub-contractors require a clear definition of what is being purchased and the terms of the agreement. We are amazed how much is assumed in a good relationship between a company and its supplier. Such an arrangement is fine—until another supplier is needed. Then problems are apt to start.

The solution is to have a definitive description of what is to be provided. This can be in the form of a drawing or specification. When the requirements can be defined by referencing a catalogue or part number, there is no need to provide a drawing or specification.

> *For years a company had bought components from a supplier and had experienced no problems using the items in an assembly process. When the company was sold, the new owners decided to produce the components in house. Everything was made to drawing, but the items did not fit properly and could not be used. After much analysis, the new owners learned that over the years the supplier and customer had adjusted the design of the components to make them work. The adjustments were never mentioned in subsequent orders or reflected in any of the drawings.*

Operations

"Operations" is defined as the main activity in which a company makes its money. Examples include: *production* in manufacturing, *teaching* in a school, *recruitment* in an employment agency, and *food preparation* in a restaurant. These activities are well controlled in successful companies. Two aspects that often require attention are records of the work being done and verification that requirements have been met.

Verification does not mean an independent inspection of an operator's work. It is totally acceptable for the person who is doing the work to confirm and record that it has been done to specification and that variations from specifications have been recorded. Independent inspection does not conform to modern quality philosophies nor is it a requirement of the ISO 9000 Standard.

Where equipment is used to measure the features and characteristics of the product or service, its accuracy needs to be established. All calibrations, whether in-house or an outside service, must be traceable to national standards.

It is usually unnecessary to write many new work instructions for this area. Where needed, they usually already exist as drawings, set-up sheets, recipes, manuals, and test specifications.

Human Resources

The human resource function is generally responsible for the training requirements of ISO 9000. The Standard requires that an organization establish and maintain training records that demonstrate the level of experience and training of all employees. Because the need for work instructions is related to their knowledge and skill levels, objective evidence of their qualifications is necessary.

To fulfill the requirement for training records, a data base of existing employees must be established. Employees can provide the data by completing a simple questionnaire showing all the training they have received, both within the company and elsewhere. Where major qualifications exist, it is a good idea to attach to the employee's record, a copy of the certificate or diploma.

Once the initial records are established, they should be periodically reviewed to identify employees needing additional training. There must be a training record for every employee, even the chief executive. Because auditors often ask to see training records, it is a good idea to keep them separated from the personnel files containing confidential information.

Most auditors check the training records to verify that all employees have had quality awareness training that included a discussion of the company's quality policy. This training is a specific requirement of the Standard. Auditors also like to check for proof that the internal auditors have been trained. Other training records the auditors might ask to see are those involving legal requirements such as proper drivers' licenses. Otherwise, auditors usually let the company decide on what training is needed.

Finance

Although finance is not directly addressed by the Standard, the financial function is involved in all aspects of the registration effort through budgeting and allocating funds. If the company does not have defined terms and conditions for procurement and sales, the finance department should work with sales and purchasing to develop them. Finance department employees are particularly well suited to do internal audits because of their training and separation from the company's main operations.

Summary

This chapter defined management's role in the registration process. Chapter 6 offers a more detailed, nine-step plan for achieving registration. The activities described therein are normally carried out by the implementation team, but management has a role throughout.

In Chapter Two, we identified three general requirements for registration to ISO 9000:

- define and document a quality system that satisfies the requirements of the Standard,
- implement and use that system as documented, and
- operate the system, and produce records that demonstrate the effectiveness of the quality system.

This chapter translates these requirements into the steps, activities, and outputs necessary to achieve registration efficiently and effectively. We discuss what must be done and why each step is important.

Chapter 6

What Needs to Be Done

In This Chapter:

- Nine Steps Leading to ISO 9000 Registration

    Phase A • Analyze and Evaluate Existing Processes
    1. Prepare for the project.
    2. Analyze and evaluate existing processes.

    Phase B • Optimize and Document the Quality System
    3. Optimize the processes.
    4. Document and approve the quality system.

    Phase C • Implement, Operate, Refine the Quality System
    5. Train internal auditors and prepare to operate the system.
    6. Operate and refine the documented system.
    7. Verify readiness.

    Phase D • Registrar Audit and Registration
    8. Prepare for the registration audit.
    9. Registration audit and registration.

- After Registration
    • Surveillance Audits
    • Operating the Quality System

Step 1
Prepare for the Project

The ISO 9000 registration process should not be traumatic if the present quality system meets customer needs and expectations. All organizations already have a quality system, although it may not be formalized and documented.

In Chapter 4 we discussed the key decisions that must be made before the project begins. These concerned the approach to registration, project organization, staff selection, and the use of outside resources. The project team must be selected and trained, employees alerted to the decision, outside resources hired, and a plan for implementation developed.

Training

All employees need some knowledge of ISO 9000 and the registration process. Management and the implementation team require special training for their leadership roles. Other employees need to understand what ISO 9000 is and how registration will affect them. Training programs, with separate, defined objectives for different employee groups, are scheduled throughout the project. Training requirements were discussed in Chapter 4.

Management

The management team, comprising both executive and line management, is the first and most important group to be trained. The training covers:

- ISO 9000 Standards, their contents and objectives,
- management's role,
- the ISO 9000 registration process,
- the benefits of ISO 9000, and
- the effects of registration on management's work and areas of responsibility.

The management team should be trained as a group. Implementing ISO 9000 requires teamwork, and team members must agree on the scope of the project and the approach they will take.

Management training can be done several ways. One method is for managers to study this book, discuss its content, and come to a common and informed understanding of ISO 9000 and the required effort.

Another approach is to have a consultant lead the training sessions. The advantage here is that managers can interact with an outside expert. Alternatively, an internal expert could lead the training sessions. This, of course, would be limited by the knowledge and ability of the internal expert.

Implementation Team

The implementation team was introduced in Chapter 4 (see Figure 4.3 on page 71). Because the team is responsible for attaining registration, its members need the most training. They must understand the ISO 9000 Standard and its registration requirements and learn how to document and operate a quality system. Documenting the quality system is, by far, the team's biggest task.

By the end of their training, implementation team members must be able to:

- apply the ISO 9000 requirements to the organization,
- analyze and define processes using flow charts and other tools,
- identify current operating inefficiencies and implement improvements,
- identify deficiencies against the Standard and eliminate them in an optimal way,
- document the processes used by the organization as procedures,
- write required work instructions, and
- prepare a quality manual.

111

The training for the implementation team is extensive and must be done by experienced providers. It is critical that the team understand and agree upon strategy and approach to registration. Too often an organization sends team members to more than one course, each espousing its own approach to registration. This often results in time wasted as team members argue over which approach to use. To avoid this, it is best to train the entire team as a group.

Employee Awareness

Registration is an accomplishment of the entire organization. For their involvement, employees don't need an extensive understanding of ISO 9000. They can be trained using simple presentations. Material for use in these sessions can either be purchased or developed by the implementation team.

The communication model in Chapter 5 gives the timing and content of communications to employees.

Project Plan

Achieving ISO 9000 registration is a significant accomplishment for any organization. It is a major project, even for organizations with established quality policies and procedures. An implementation plan is needed. Progress can then be monitored and controlled through registration.

The starting point for the plan is the desired registration date. After that, intermediate steps and milestones can be determined and scheduled back to the start. To effectively control and monitor the plan, an appropriate number of milestones and sub-tasks must be assigned. Appendix C contains sample plans taking eight, twelve, and eighteen-months to achieve registration.

The project plan is not something to be developed and then placed in a drawer. Executive managers should review the progress of the project against the plan every month. This will provide control and enforce discipline to ensure that registration and other objectives are met. Managing the implementation is good training for forthcoming management reviews which are required by the Standard.

Step 2
Analyze and Evaluate Existing Processes

The introduction to ISO 9001 says:

"The design and implementation of a quality system will be influenced by the varying needs of an organization, its particular objectives, the products and services supplied, and the processes and specific practices employed."

The Standard recognizes that a quality system must be unique to an organization in order to reflect its operations. This implies that before the system can be designed, current practices must be fully analyzed and understood. Existing practices have been defined by the needs of the business operating in its present environment. If the business is successful, existing practices are apparently adequate, making them a good place to start. Implementing a new system without understanding the current one invites disaster.

Businesses use processes to achieve their objectives, and those processes make up the quality system. Procedures describe the processes. The Standard requires effective management of processes, but it leaves the "how-to" up to the organization. It does identify the features and characteristics of a sound management system.

A cake can be described quite easily. Its flavor and texture can be identified, and the color, flavor, and thickness of the icing noted. Its dimensions and shape can be measured as well. A cake can be made quite easily by following the same processes the baker uses. Cakes with the same features and characteristics can be made time

113

and time again. The key is process management. To begin, a process needs to be defined and controlled. To make a cake, the controlled process must include details such as ingredients and their quantities, the order in which they are added, mixing method, pan preparation and size, and cooking time and temperature.

An organization must have many processes in order to operate its business. And its primary business is, of necessity, finding and keeping customers. The cycle begins with the customer's order and ends with delivery of the product or service. To support these operational processes, the quality system needs organizational processes. These include activities such as management review, computer system back-up, calibration, and addressing customer complaints.

A process, by definition, adds value to the product or service. It is important that organizations analyze and understand how each process works. If improvements can be made in efficiency, control, or customer satisfaction, a process should be changed. With careful examination, it is rare to find one that cannot be improved.

The analysis of an existing process can reveal amazing things, as we learned while examining a client's invoicing process. The Manager told us how it worked: sales information was entered, and the system updated accounts and produced invoices. Simple, right?

When we started to investigate, we became entangled in a case of industrial archaeology. Six generations of systems were still being faithfully followed, the oldest requiring manual entries in a ledger. Each time a new system was developed, it was piggybacked onto the original system, "just in case the new system doesn't work." But when the new system did work, no one told the invoice clerk to stop using the old one. Once the "dig" was sorted out, the clerk was released from many meaningless tasks.

Each process should be evaluated against the requirements of the Standard. Identified shortfalls must be addressed.

Figure 6.1 shows the operational processes of a training and consulting firm. Figure 6.2 (page 118) shows the processes organized into procedures.

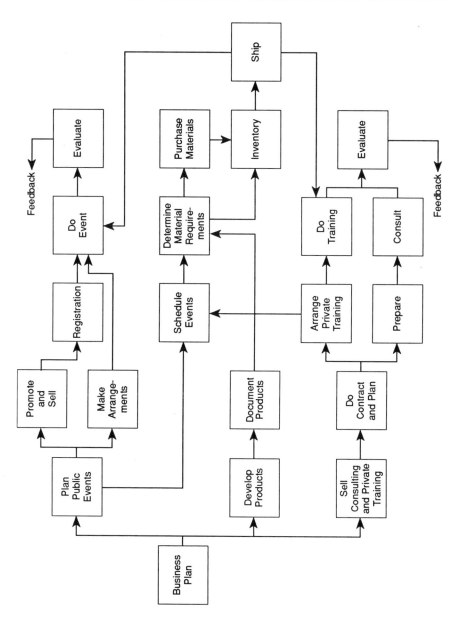

Figure 6.1   Major Processes:
Training and Consulting Firm

Step 3
Optimize the Processes

By the time you identify, understand, and evaluate present processes, you may feel ready to document them as procedures. It's tempting, but first you need to determine whether the current processes and systems are what the business needs. It may be the time for serious process analysis, improvement, or even reengineering.

Reengineering means starting with a clean slate. Ask yourself what you would do differently if you were starting from scratch. Even if a reengineering recommendation cannot be implemented today, it could be a goal to aim for in the future. You are the one who knows what is achievable in the present environment.

In most organizations there is at least one process that can be modified to produce savings. Usually there is more than one. The savings can be substantial—sometimes enough to pay for the entire ISO 9000 registration project.

> *A real estate agency used its computer system to list and describe all available properties. The staff in one office used the system to draw up listing agreements for prospective sellers prior to visiting their homes. It was no surprise when that office staff achieved a high rate of new listings. The sales staff in another of the agency's offices prepared the listing agreement only after a seller had decided to use their services. After adopting the first practice as a company standard, the agency noted a marked improvement in its overall performance as well as in the services it provided its customers.*

Unless the person optimizing the process has a good understanding of the meaning of the Standard, there is potential for inappropriate changes. Fortunately that potential is small. The Standard is practical, and its requirements are no more than sound business practices. Removing deficiencies against the Standard normally improves long-term operations.

Step 4
Document and Approve the Quality System

Section 4.2 of the Standard says:

> "The supplier shall establish, document, and maintain a quality system as a means of ensuring that product conforms to specified requirements. The supplier shall prepare a quality manual covering the requirements of this International Standard. The quality manual shall include or make reference to the quality systems procedures and outline the structure of the documentation used in the quality system."

The Standard further states that the supplier shall "prepare documented procedures consistent with the requirements of this International Standard and the supplier's stated quality policy." In other words, registered organizations need a documented quality system that includes a quality manual, procedures, and work instructions.

These three levels of documentation are interrelated. The Quality Manual contains the quality policy. The procedures describe how the policy is achieved and reference work instructions. Together the three comprise the documented quality system. We recommend that the documentation be prepared in this order: procedures, work instructions, and quality manual.

Procedures

Throughout the Standard, you will find, "The supplier shall establish and maintain procedures to... ." "The supplier" is the organization seeking registration (you), and "shall" means you must do as it says.

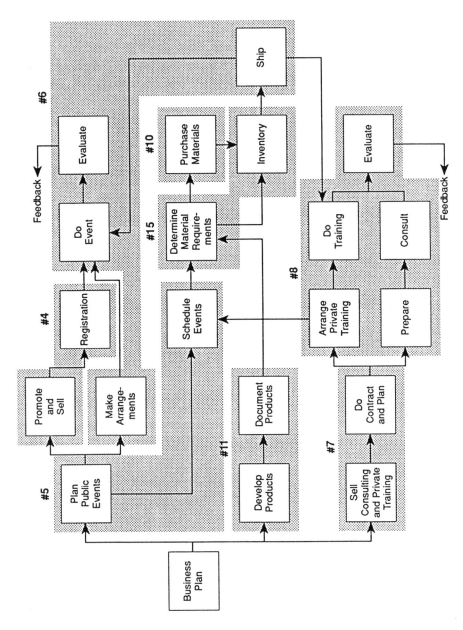

Figure 6.2   Operational Procedures:
Training and Consulting Firm

Procedures are the heart of the quality system. They describe the processes the organization uses to identify, define and meet the needs and requirements of its customers. Processes should be grouped together and documented for meaningful procedures, ignoring functional boundaries. Figures 6.2 (page 118) and 6.3 below show how this has been applied to the consulting and training firm introduced in Figure 6.1 (page 115).

Selling	*Delivering*		*Ensuring*
Sale of Client Services 7	Delivery of Client Svcs 8	Training 13	Control of Complaints 12
Sale of Public Events 4	Delivery Public Events 6	Planning Public Events 5	Control of Manuals 1
Inquiries 14	Purchasing 10	Supplier Approval 9	Quality Audit 2
	Product Dev 11	Inventory Control 15	Mgmt Review and Corrective Action 3

Figure 6.3   List of Procedures: Training and Consulting Firm

Procedures define the means to control processes. A procedure needs to clearly state the objective, assign responsibilities for the completion of the work, identify the documents used and records kept, and describe what needs to be done.

Once implemented, procedures improve the control of processes, ensure a more consistent performance, and allow everyone to understand how processes are performed.

Procedures should be written, tested, and finalized as they are documented (Figure 6.4, page 120). Remember—the purpose of the procedures is to provide guidance and instruction to employees.

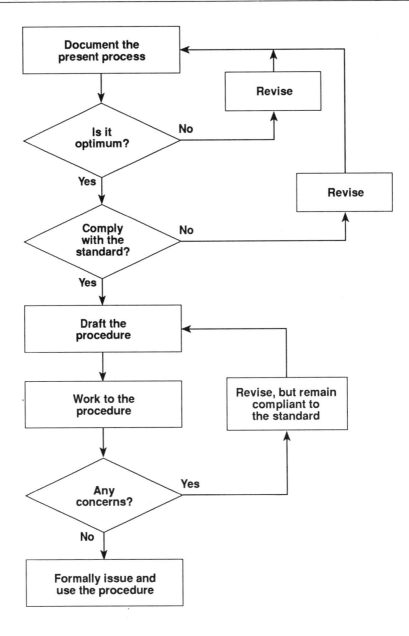

Figure 6.4   Procedure Writing

Procedures should be clear, understandable, and user-friendly. When employees help develop procedures, they usually understand and use them. Appendix E illustrates procedure format and detail.

The names used to identify functions and processes are unique to the organization; procedures should use the same terminology. If the organization calls purchasing "procurement," call it that. There is little reason to adopt the terminology of the Standard.

The team who is writing procedures determine whether employees need additional guidance—*i.e.,* work instructions.

Work Instructions

The Standard states that the level of documentation is dependent on the complexity of the work, the methods used, and the skills and training needed by the personnel involved in carrying out the activity. This is a very broad guideline. The Standard expects organizations to perform work consistently. Hence, the need for work instructions depends on the qualifications of the employees performing a job. Most employees can carry out their tasks without instructions telling them "how."

Clearly nobody would suggest that clerks require instructions telling them how to write, or drivers, how to steer a vehicle. We all accept the premise that some activities are within the known capabilities of the employee, whether acquired by training or experience. The bottom line is that you need "how to" instructions only when they are necessary to ensure that the task gets done correctly, completely, and consistently.

If work instructions are necessary, they probably already exist. Operating businesses know where instructions are needed to help employees do their jobs. If employees do their work successfully without instructions, ISO 9000 registration does not require them. In conclusion, you should not need to write many work instructions.

Once procedures and work instructions have been written and approved, start using them without delay. If procedures are based on existing practices, implementation should not be difficult except when there are changes and new activities to be initiated.

Quality Manual

The quality manual includes the quality policy and explains how the quality system satisfies the Standard's requirements. Auditors want to see this before scheduling an audit or pre-audit visit.

The quality manual is best formatted by section of the Standard. It also needs to articulate how the organization's procedures relate to the Standard's requirements. The typical quality manual contains between ten and twenty-five pages. The quality manual is not an operating document and does not change very often. Some organizations use it for marketing.

Sometimes the staff of an organization writes the quality manual as the first activity in the documentation phase. They argue that the first task is to determine how to satisfy the Standard. This is then documented as the quality manual, which becomes the basis for writing procedures.

We disagree. We think that the quality manual should be written last. As explained earlier, we start with how the organization operates and check for compliance as processes are analyzed, optimized, and documented.

The procedures and related work instructions define the quality system. When they are complete, it is a simple matter to write the quality manual. The quality manual is normally written by the project leader, Management Representative for Quality, a consultant, and/or the implementation team.

The quality manual, procedures, and work instructions are all products of the "document-the-quality-system" step. They should be distributed, as needed, to employees doing the work.

This completes "Phase B — Optimize and document the quality system." But don't breathe a sigh of relief just yet. The reality is that you never finish Phase B. You should be continually on the look-out for changes you can make that will improve the system—in order to improve the business. However, at this point it is time to move into Phase C — "Implement, operate and refine the quality system."

Step 5
Train Internal Auditors and
Prepare to Operate the System

Operating the quality system means running the business as documented. While continuing much of what you already do, you are initiating internal audits, management reviews, and other processes—new activities for most organizations.

In the previous section we recommended implementing procedures and work instructions as they are completed and verified. This makes sense. You certainly don't want to finalize a procedure and then say, "This is a new procedure, but don't use it yet."

Implementing the quality system requires:

- developing an internal audit program,
- formally authorizing and issuing all documentation,
- communicating with the work force, and
- training the work force.

Internal Auditing Program

Internal auditing is the systematic assessment of the use and effectiveness of the organization's quality system. Audit results are reported and identify noncompliances. Corrective actions are then developed to bring the operation back into line with the documented quality system or to improve the system.

Internal auditing is not concerned with whether the documented quality system complies with the ISO 9000 Standard. Rather, its concern is whether the system is being implemented as documented. Compliance to the Standard is designed into the quality system as it is developed and documented.

The requirement to carry out internal audits is established in ISO 9000, Section 4.17, which states:

> "The supplier shall establish and maintain documented procedures for planning and implementing internal quality audits to verify whether quality activities and related results comply with planned arrangements and to determine the effectiveness of the quality system."

"The supplier" is the organization seeking registration; "quality activities" are how the business operates; "planned arrangements" refer to the documented quality system. An internal auditing program requires:

- an internal auditing procedure,
- an audit schedule, and
- qualified auditors.

Internal Auditing Procedure

As the Standard indicates, "a procedure to plan and implement internal quality audits is needed." This procedure is part of the documented quality system.

Audit Schedule

The internal auditing procedure defines how often the quality system is audited and the qualifications of internal auditors. The most effective internal auditing programs are based on the following premises:

• Procedures describe the quality system. It is best to schedule internal audits by procedure, as discussed in Chapter 4. If all procedures are audited for all parts of the business, the entire quality system is audited.

• The entire quality system should be audited every six months, on average. Some procedures may be problematic, requiring more attention. Others can be audited less frequently. All procedures should be audited at least annually, and these audits should be spread out over the year.

• One person can carry out an effective internal audit, but auditors may be teamed up, especially in the beginning.

• The preparation, conduct, and completion of an internal audit takes no more than half a day.

Qualified Internal Auditors

You must decide on the size and composition of your internal audit team. The size will depend on the number and scope of your procedures, the number of auditors per audit, and the number of audits each auditor will do.

Internal audits are conducted by employee-auditors who have received formal training. Auditors must be independent of the process being audited. The audit team should include senior-level managers, other managers, professionals, and non-professional employees. Senior management involvement sends a positive message about its commitment to quality and ISO 9000. Senior-level people find internal auditing interesting and enjoy "getting out of the office." However, it is important to reemphasize that rank has no place in internal auditing. No matter their position, internal auditors are only internal auditors when conducting audits.

The Standard does not set specific requirements for the kind of training internal auditors must have, but registrars generally ask to see documented evidence that the audits have been conducted by people trained to do internal auditing.

Internal auditing strategy was discussed in Chapter 4, and the role of executive management in internal auditing in Chapter 5.

Issuing the Documentation

The documented quality system is not complete until documents have been reviewed and approved. Procedures, work instructions, and manuals should be distributed so they are easily accessible to those who need them. Not everyone will need a copy.

Only the latest documents can be in circulation. When a new version comes out, old documents must be retrieved, destroyed, and replaced. Documents should be distributed only where they are required, and records must be kept of who has them. Your document control procedure describes the process for accomplishing this.

Communicating with the Work Force

Before operation begins, employees should be fully informed. Everyone needs to know that operating the system means working to procedures and work instructions. The communication should stress the importance of doing exactly what is specified, with particular emphasis on completing specified paperwork. This communication is also an opportunity to introduce or reinforce the quality policy and objectives, and it should be two-way to allow for discussion and feedback. Chapter 5 contains additional information on this communication with the work force.

Training the Work Force

Employees need to be prepared to operate the new and modified processes that result from improvements and changes made to comply with the Standard. These are usually minor, affecting only a small number of employees. We recommend that these changes be implemented as soon as they are agreed upon and the affected staff can be trained. This is a low-key approach which allows the implementation to occur with minimal disruption.

Some employees will need to learn the new activities that are required to meet the Standard, and they must be trained. The processes discussed in the procedures must be explained; then, each process must be monitored as it is performed.

Throughout, all employees need to know exactly what is required of them. They must understand the procedures and work instructions that guide their work. And they must know where the documents that describe their work are kept.

When the system is documented and the employees trained, the official operation of the quality system can begin.

Step 6
Operate the Quality System

Once the quality system is in operation, employees will need time prior to the registrar audit to "iron out the wrinkles." This is the time to "fine-tune" the system. Registrars look for evidence of system effectiveness. Where there have been major changes in procedures, three to six months may be required to achieve the looked-for level of effectiveness. Where the processes have changed little, existing records can often provide the evidence without further ado.

In addition to current work, operating the quality system now means performing new activities as well. These new activtities usually include:

- internal audits (see the above discussion),
- management reviews, where management meets to review the operating results of the system,
- formal corrective and preventive actions, which fix deficiencies in the system and find and eliminate their causes, and
- document control, that removes all obsolete documents from circulation.

Operating an ISO 9000 quality system requires deliberation and discipline. Records need to be completed and signed. All corrective actions must be completed and their effectiveness verified.

When the Process Management Approach is used, implementation is not particularly difficult. You are not implementing a foreign system. Your new ISO 9000-compliant system is similar to what you had, and it has been designed just for your business. Much of what the Standard requires is already in place.

One aspect of the Standard that can cause problems in implementation is the calibration of measuring equipment. Where equipment is used to measure the characteristics of a product or service, the accuracy of the equipment must be established.

Most scales of measurement, such as weight, distance, temperature, and time, have known standards. Instruments are checked against these standards, which are traced to a national or international standard. This external reference is important; measurements must be correct to prevent problems for customers.

There is a story of a general who was visiting a fort in western Canada. The fort had a long-established tradition of firing a gun at midday so that the settlers would know the time. The general was a stickler for tradition and wanted to check his own pocket watch. He went out onto the parade ground at five minutes to noon and waited. But noon came, and nothing happened. Finally, at two minutes past noon, a soldier came out and fired the gun. The general checked out the system and found that there was a chronometer in the guard room that was used by the sergeant to give the order to the soldier. The general asked the sergeant how he checked the accuracy of the chronometer and was told that once a month it was taken into town, where a clocksmith checked it against his own chronometer and adjusted it as necessary. The sergeant even showed the general the book in which the time checks were recorded.

Later that day the general was in town and stopped to see the clocksmith. The routine was confirmed. The young clocksmith proudly told him how the tradition went back to his grandfather. His grandfather made a journey once a year to the state capital to check out the chronometer. In his father's day this was replaced by a telephone call. He went on to say that he had dispensed with this expense when he found that the noonday gun at the fort was so accurate it always agreed with his chronometer!

Calibration to a standard outside the system is needed. The calibration masters must be checked by a service whose measurements can be traced to the national or international standards. You do not want a noonday gun scenario!

During the operating phase, and prior to the registrar audit, you will need to:

- conduct at least two complete internal audits of the system,
- hold at least two management reviews,
- demonstrate how you initiate and carry out corrective and preventive actions, and
- generate sufficient records to demonstrate the operation and effectiveness of the quality system.

You will implement the changes needed to improve your system, making sure the changes don't take the system out of compliance with the Standard.

Step 7
Verify Readiness

In Chapter 4, we discussed pre-assessment audits. We recommended that while you need to verify your readiness, you need not hire someone to do a pre-assessment audit. Many organizations, however, hire someone to conduct a pre-assessment audit, believing it will help them prepare for the final audit.

If you plan to hire someone to do the readiness check, we suggest that you choose your registrar or an experienced consultant.

If you choose your registrar, ask that the same auditor do both the pre-assessment and final audit. That way, you shouldn't have too many surprises during the final audit. To allow enough time to fix noncompliances, the pre-assessment audit should be scheduled at least four weeks before assessment. If major concerns are found, then the assessment date can be rescheduled.

Step 8
Prepare for the Registration Audit

By the time the auditors arrive for the audit, they will have reviewed some of your documentation and may have toured your facility as well. During the audit, they will verify that:

- your quality system meets the ISO 9000 requirements,
- you are using the system as documented, and
- the system is effectively meeting customer requirements.

For the audit:

- Make sure all employees know when the audit will be held. Tell them what to expect and how to respond to questions. Most employees will not be interviewed by an auditor. Those who are should answer questions honestly. The main job for everyone is to continue working according to the quality system.

- Remind employees of the quality policy—increase their awareness of quality.

- Be sure all executives and other key management personnel are present for the audit. Their presence confirms a commitment to quality and to ISO 9000 registration.

- Look sharp. Perception is always important. Dispose of old equipment, files, and supplies that are not needed. Clean up the facility and dust any idle equipment. When the facility looks sharp, employees are more confident, and the auditors will perceive that yours is a quality organization.

• Organize all records and make sure they are retrievable and complete. Much of the auditor's time is spent examining records.

The auditors are professionals who are experienced in organization assessment. No matter how prepared you are, they will still find some noncompliances. But thorough preparation will reduce the number.

Step 9
Registration Audit and Registration

The big day has arrived. If you have made a committed effort and invested the necessary resources, you have nothing to worry about. Most companies get registered. The auditors always find some noncompliances, but you will have the opportunity to correct them. When the noncompliances are cleared, your registration is granted.

Your goal should be to have only minor noncompliances that can be cleared without another visit by the auditors. In-person verification of fixes is expensive and opens you up to the possibility of additional findings. It is far better to clear noncompliances by mail.

The audit will start with an opening meeting at which the auditor will explain the ground rules. It is essential that all senior management is present. You only have one opportunity to make a first impression—don't spoil it.

The auditors will request guides to accompany them throughout the audit. The guides should be employees who know the quality system. Their purpose is to ensure that the auditors are given the information and answers they seek. Knowledgeable guides can reduce the number of noncompliances; other employees can unintentionally give incomplete or incorrect answers.

The auditors will document noncompliances and review them with you as the audit proceeds. You should have the right people available to make changes and clear noncompliances. But remember, the auditors are not interested in quick fixes. They want to see genuine corrective actions that eliminate causes of noncompliances.

> *An incomplete record is a non-compliance. Going through the file and completing all records is not an acceptable corrective action. It only fixes a past practice and current situation. An acceptable corrective action in this situation is to train the employees who produce the records. Another acceptable solution is to provide better instructions to ensure that employees keep complete records.*

At the end of the audit you will know if you will be recommended for registration. The auditors tell you what noncompliances they have found and how long you have to clear them. Once they are cleared, you are recommended for registration. This may seem like the end of the journey, but it is not. Once you attain registration, you are telling the world you have a system that continually seeks to improve the business and quality of products and services. After registration is when the benefits start accruing.

After Registration

Some say quality is a journey without end. If so, then ISO 9000 registration is a commitment without end. Registration is not the end but the beginning—the first major event on the path to improved performance.

Through internal auditing, management review, and corrective and preventive actions, an ISO 9000-registered quality system commits the organization to seek ways to improve. The ISO 9000 assessment process, through the ongoing surveillance audits, verifies that the commitment is real.

Surveillance Audits

All registrars perform surveillance audits. They are usually planned well in advance, and their purpose is to confirm that the system is still in place and effective, not to see if the organization is out of compliance. The frequency of surveillance audits depends on the health of a quality system and policy of the registrar; the norm is every six months. A registrar will probably schedule more frequent audits if a system barely passed the registration audit or if concerns were found at an earlier surveillance audit.

Some registrars offer smaller companies a program that enables them to maintain registration with only an annual surveillance visit. Sometimes the company is asked to send its internal audit reports and other information every six months for examination. Such an arrangement reduces the cost of maintaining registration, yet ensures a sufficient level of control.

In addition to surveillance audits, many registrars re-assess the entire system at the end of the three- or four-year registration period. Their rationale is that surveillance visits do not examine the complete system—just parts of it. Some registrars, however, feel the surveillance audits are sufficient to continue the registration.

The initial surveillance visit is often the time when the quality system faces its first true test. Organizations often make last-minute adjustments to their systems, just prior to the initial registration audit, to ensure that everything will be ready for inspection. The soundness (or lack thereof) of these last minute changes may not be apparent during the registration audit.

However, by the first surveillance audit, the viability of these fixes may have become more apparent. If management has relaxed and shifted its focus elsewhere, and internal auditors have not detected the shortcomings, the organization could be embarrassed by what the auditors uncover.

Noncompliances do not automatically lead to the loss of registration, but effective corrective action is necessary. Noncompliances could require an extra surveillance visit from the registrar at additional cost and wasted management time. Usually the concerns are sufficiently minor to be left to the next surveillance audit. Either way they must be addressed. If noncompliances are not fixed, registration is withdrawn, and the organization has the unpleasant task of informing its customers.

If an organization is operating its quality system as documented, it should be able to withstand examination at any time. Special preparation for a surveillance audit should not be necessary —apart from telling employees when it will be and ensuring that key staff members are available. The surveillance is to confirm that the system is in place and improving the organization's performance.

During a surveillance audit, there are some key aspects of the system that are always examined. They are internal audits, management reviews, and corrective and preventive actions. If these are being addressed properly, the auditor will have confidence in the rest of the system. The converse is also true.

Sometimes a surveillance visit will be conducted by a new auditor not familiar with the business. The new auditor should not "move the goal posts." If the original assessment approved a major feature of the documented quality system, it cannot suddenly become unacceptable. An organization should never have to make fundamental changes to meet the whims of an individual auditor.

> *One of our earliest clients was a small company doing plating for local manufacturing companies. There were only seven employees, counting the chief executive, who often took off his jacket, put on his jeans, and helped operate the plating line.*
>
> *The company's documented quality system met its needs, controlled its processes, and achieved ISO 9000 registration. Everyone understood the system and worked as a team. Everyone accepted responsibility for ensuring that the customers' needs and expectations were met, and customers rarely complained. The system worked.*
>
> *Then, a "total quality expert" was assigned to a surveillance audit. He believed that because quality is about continual improve-*

ment, a quality system that did not demonstrate evidence of change could not be meeting its objectives. He "found" noncompliances in order to promote change.

The chief executive came to us for help. We talked with the registrar's management, something he was afraid to do, and another auditor was sent to re-appraise the situation. The re-assessment found that the system was achieving the requirements of the Standard, was producing improvements, and was allowing the organization to control its quality. But the company's relationship with the registrar was permanently damaged. Once the genuine noncompliances were cleared, the company found another registrar.

You and your registrar should have a relationship built on support and assistance, not fault-finding and conflict. You are the customer, and the registrar should be meeting your needs and expectations. If this is not happening, find out why. The registrar needs to know your concerns in order to take corrective action. If you still aren't satisfied, it's probably time to hire a new registrar.

Operating the Quality System

Prior to registration, you started operating the quality system. *Operating the quality system*, as shown in Figure 6.5 (page 136), means running the business as documented, performing internal audits, holding management reviews, and taking corrective action.

Operating the quality system means improving quality and performance. Operating the business means bettering the business's competitive position. The improvements and benefits will accumulate if the design and implementation of the quality system are done correctly and if management fulfills its role.

Summary

This chapter summarized the steps required to achieve registration. They are usually carried out by an implementation team that involves almost everyone in the organization. As it was explained in

Chapter 4, management has overall responsibility for attaining the certificate and doing so with a system that adds value to the organization. Management must participate and lead through all steps of the registration effort.

As we said earlier, registration is not the end. Maintaining registration requires continued operation and ongoing registrar assessment.

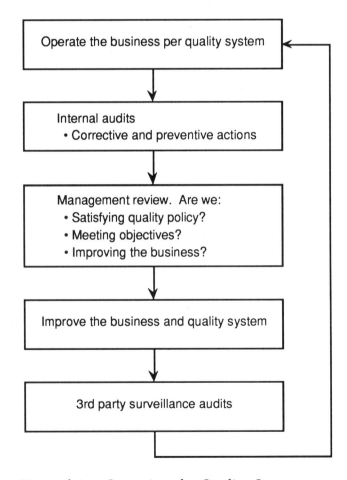

Figure 6.5   Operating the Quality System

The contents of this book have indicated why registration to ISO 9000 can be a rewarding experience for an organization.

It makes the case that these benefits will not be achieved without management commitment and involvement.

Chapter 7 summarizes the role of management in a chart—which indicates the management role at each step of the project and the decisions that must be made.

It also provides a simple cross reference to the rest of the book.

Chapter 7

ISO 9000 Registration and More

In This Chapter:

- A review of management's role and key decisions to ensure more than the registration certificate

Organizations decide to pursue ISO 9000 registration for a variety of reasons. A customer suggests or even requires it; others are doing it; the quality staff sees it as a challenge. Perhaps the sales department is looking for a competitive advantage or executives may view it as a strategic initiative. Whatever the reason, the decision belongs to management.

Once the decision to pursue ISO 9000 registration is made, many executives simply leave the project to the implementation team. They provide the team with targets and a budget and a "Let me know when I can help... ." If asked, they approve the quality policy, review the progress and make the right noises at communication meetings. Eventually the project is completed and ISO 9000 registration is achieved. But what is left on the table?

There can and should be more from the ISO 9000 registration, but for these greater benefits to be obtained the executive management need be involved. Understanding the nature of these benefits and ensuring they are realized is the responsibility of the executive management.

ISO 9000 is about the management of quality, and that means the management of the whole company. It is too important to be left to quality specialists who do not necessarily have a holistic view of the organization. It needs top management participation in the registration process and the subsequent operation of the Quality System.

The message of this book is that there is much more to ISO 9000 than the registration certificate for the wall. The process of getting registered—and registration itself—can yield huge benefits for the organization. ISO 9000 must lead to a business that operates better, is more competitive, and has more satisfied customers. Management's job is to ensure that the "extra" benefits are realized.

We conclude this book with a table that summarizes what is needed for your organization to reap these "extras." The following table recaps the previous six chapters and indicates key management decisions and roles from the decision to seek registration, on through the process, and on to registration itself. The table is organized by the steps in the process so that you can conveniently refer to it as your registration effort progresses.

Our hope is that this book makes you want more from ISO 9000 and helps you make the choices and take the actions necessary to get more.

For convenient usage, the table begins on page 142.

Registration Process	Management Role	Management Decisions	Chapter Reference
The ISO 9000 decision.		The decision to pursue ISO 9000 registration is management's. Chapters 1-3 provide information on costs and benefits.	1, 2, 3
Yes, go for it.	Communicate the decision to the organization.	Management, at this point, should not turn the project over to staff. There are a number of important decisions to be made that impact achieving registration and, more importantly, the benefits that result. These decisions include:	5
		1) Using an approach that provides an optimum quality system. The authors recommend the Process Management Approach.	4
		2) Setting objectives for more than registration itself.	4
		3) Determining the scope of the registration.	4
		4) Determining need for and, if needed, selecting outside resources.	4
		5) Organizing the effort.	4
		6) Selecting and organizing internal resources.	4
		7) Appointing a Project Leader and the Management Representative for Quality.	4
	Lead the writing of a quality policy and quality objectives.	8) Selecting and hiring a registrar.	4 5

The steps to ISO 9000 registration.

Steps		
Phase A *Analyze and evaluate existing processes.*		
1) Prepare for the project. a) Training	Learn about ISO 9000 and what is required to get registered.	Approve the organization training plan. — 2, 6
b) Project plan		Approve the project plan and budget. — 4, 6
2) Analyze and evaluate existing processes.	Objectively examine performance of existing processes.	— 3, 6
Phase B *Optimize and document the quality system.*		
3) Optimize the processes.		Determine the need for improving and/or reengineering processes. — 3, 6
4) Document and approve the quality system.	Become familiar with the quality system.	Approve part of the quality system as required. — 2, 6
Phase C *Implement, operate and refine the quality system.*		
5) Train internal auditors and prepare for operation of the quality system. a) Communicate with the work force.	Communicate to all employees on the shift from the documentation phase to the operating phase.	— 5, 6
b) Internal auditing program.	Become trained and part of the internal audit team.	Approve an internal auditing strategy that audits by procedure and uses a cross-functional audit team from all levels of the organization. — 5, 6

Registration Process	Management Role	Management Decisions	Chapter Reference
6) Operate and refine the quality system.	Perform activities as specified in the quality system: • Conduct management reviews • Perform internal audits		5, 6
7) Verify readiness.		Decide when and who will do a readiness check.	4, 6
Phase D *Registrar audit and registration.*			
8) Prepare for the registrar audit.	Ensure that all executives and key staff are available for the registrar audit.		6
	Communicate the details of the registration audit to all employees.		5, 6
9) Registrar audit and registration.	Actively participate in opening and closing meetings. Sell the organization's quality system, quality results and commitment to quality to auditors in opening meeting.		6
	Meet with auditors for management's portion of the quality system.		6
	Communicate the positive outcome to all employees.		5, 6

After registration.		
Surveillance audits	Be available and participate in surveillance audits as required.		6
	Ensure the organization responds to auditor feedback.		6
Operating the quality system.	Through management reviews, ensure the continued operation and improvement of the quality system and the business.		5
	Set objectives and measure the return from the ISO 9000 investment.		3
	Use ISO 9000 as a platform for a more comprehensive quality program.	Consider expanding ISO 9000 to other parts of the business for a more comprehensive quality program.	3
			3
	Maximize the marketing potential of ISO 9000 registration.	Consider managing and organizing the business by process.	3
			3

Appendix A
ISO 9000 Compliance Check

ISO 9000 prescribes requirements for the quality system of an organization. It requires the quality system to be documented, to address certain issues, and to achieve certain objectives. This checklist lets you determine the extent to which your organization meets the requirements. It is general and does not attempt to address all the nuances of the Standard.

Consider each of the following questions and answer *Yes, No,* or *Partially.* Where the question does not apply to your activities, leave it blank. To meet the requirements of the Standard, you will have to answer *Yes* to all questions applicable to your business.

	Yes	No	Partially
1.0 ORGANIZATION			
1.1 Is the responsibility and authority for all activities, including the quality system, defined?			
1.2 Does executive management formally review the organization's quality performance at least every three months?			

		Yes	No	Partially
1.3	Does the organization have a quality policy that employees know and understand?			
1.4	Is there a quality manual that describes how the organization's quality system satisfies the requirements of the Standard?			
1.5	Are there up-to-date written procedures that describe the important processes used by the organization?			
1.6	Are records generated in producing a product or service that demonstrate the customer's requirements have been met? Are the records kept for a period of time that relates to the life of the product or service?			
1.7	Is the organization in compliance with applicable legislation and regulations? Are current copies of such documents kept?			
1.8	Is there a system for removing documents no longer current or relevant?			
1.9	Are internal audits done on a planned basis by trained internal auditors, independent of the function being audited?			

2.0 SALES AND MARKETING

		Yes	No	Partially
2.1	In sales agreements do both parties clearly understand the terms, conditions, and specifications of what is being bought and sold?			

		Yes	No	Partially
2.2	Are capability and capacity to fulfill an order verified before the order is accepted?			
2.3	Are the details of an order compared to the corresponding quote?			
2.4	Are contract changes agreed to in writing with the customer?			
2.5	Does a technical authority verify advertisements and technical literature used for selling?			
2.6	Does the purchase agreement cover, when applicable, the use of customer-supplied tools, materials, parts, and equipment?			

3.0 DESIGN AND DEVELOPMENT (For ISO 9001 only)

3.1	Are product requirements for all development projects defined and agreed to in writing?			
3.2	Are pertinent legislative and regulatory requirements identified and incorporated into the design requirements?			
3.3	Is there a written plan for development projects?			
3.4	Are the resources for design and development projects defined and allocated? Are the responsibilities for various activities clearly defined?			

	Yes	No	Partially

3.5 Is the progress of development projects reviewed by the stakeholders?

3.6 Is the output of the design process verified to ensure that it meets the design requirements?

3.7 Does the product documentation provide the information needed to produce/deliver the product or service?

3.8 Are all product documents approved before being issued?

3.9 When changes are made to documents, do all concerned receive revised copies, and are obsolete documents destroyed?

3.10 Are safety issues of the design identified and addressed?

3.11 Is the design validated by trials, models, prototypes, pilot runs, or similar tests?

3.12 Are alterations to the design requirements recorded and agreed to by all parties?

3.13 Is the final design formally approved and accepted by all parties?

4.0 MATERIAL MANAGEMENT

4.1 Are all materials and components that are used in producing a product or service clearly identifiable?

		Yes	No	Partially
4.2	Are all materials and components stored in a manner that prevents damage and preserves suitability for use?			
4.3	Are the requirements for procured goods clearly defined for the supplier?			
4.4	Are the organization's suppliers formally evaluated to ensure they are capable of meeting requirements?			
4.5	Are purchased goods verified upon receipt to ensure they match the order?			
4.6	Are suspect and nonconforming materials and parts prevented from being used and properly dispositioned?			
4.7	When the customer supplies items for inclusion in its product or service, is there a system to ensure that such items are protected, accounted for, and only used for that customer?			

5.0 OPERATIONS

		Yes	No	Partially
5.1	Do employees have the necessary knowledge, work aids, and instructions for the activities they perform?			
5.2	Is the equipment that is used to produce/deliver products and services analyzed to confirm it is capable of achieving the required results?			
5.3	Is there a system that defines what needs to be done and ensures it is consistently done?			

		Yes	No	Partially
5.4	Is the production status of a product or service known at all times?			
5.5	Does the organization have control over the work of subcontractors?			
5.6	Are criteria available and used to verify conformance to requirements?			
5.7	Is the equipment used to produce or deliver products and services maintained to ensure it is capable of performing as required?			
5.8	If needed, are the statistical tools used to monitor product and service characteristics?			

6.0 IMPROVING QUALITY

6.1	Are records kept of instances where a component, product, or service falls short of its requirements?			
6.2	Once problems and shortfalls are identified, are actions taken to ensure that the customer is not affected?			
6.3	When a product or service falls short of requirements, is the cause sought and addressed?			

7.0 MEASURING/TEST EQUIPMENT

7.1	Is the accuracy of measuring equipment suitable for the tolerances being measured?			

	Yes	No	Partially

7.2   Where measuring equipment is used to validate requirements, is the accuracy of the equipment maintained by a calibration program based on national standards?

7.3   Does the frequency of such calibration ensure the ongoing accuracy of the measuring equipment?

8.0   EMPLOYEE QUALIFICATIONS

8.1   Are the skills and knowledge required for each position in the organization defined?

8.2   Are the experience, qualifications, and training of employees known and recorded?

8.3   Is there a formal training program for new employees?

8.4   Are the training needs of employees routinely assessed? When found lacking, are appropriate actions taken?

8.5   Is training evaluated to ensure its objectives are being achieved?

Appendix B
A Detailed Review — ISO 9001

Quality Systems:

Model for Quality Assurance in Design, Development, Production, Installation, and Servicing

This appendix is a section-by-section review of the ISO 9001 Standard and its requirements. It can be helpful when the reader is not sure about the meaning of a particular clause of the Standard.

0.0   Introduction

The purpose of ISO 9001 and the two associated Standards, ISO 9002 and ISO 9003, is to give buyers of goods and services confidence that their suppliers meet certain external quality requirements. The ISO 9000 Standards detail the provisions of a quality system that can ensure that the buyers' requirements are agreed to and met.

It is intended that the ISO 9000 Standards be universally accepted in their present form. The Standards are generic and intended for application to the quality system of any organization. ISO Standards do not address the specifics of products and services.

A quality system that is developed to meet ISO 9000 requirements must reflect the needs of the organization, the products and services it provides, and the processes it uses. Some organizations use the ISO 9000 Standards as a basic system and introduce additional requirements for their own specific needs.

Such specifics, referred to as "technical standards," define the characteristics and requirements of products and services to be delivered to the customer. ISO Standards are meant to be complementary with technical standards.

1.0   Scope

ISO 9001 applies to organizations that design products and services. These organizations must demonstrate certain capabilities in design, development, production, and installation and service. ISO 9002 and ISO 9003 define a more limited scope. The distinction between ISO 9001 and ISO 9002 is the design capability.

2.0   Normative References

This paragraph links the ISO 9001 Standard to other ISO Standards. It encourages users of ISO 9000 to apply the most recent Standard and to incorporate other ISO Standards in developing their quality systems.

3.0   Definitions

ISO 8402 is referenced as the source for definitions when using the ISO 9000 Standards.

"Product," as used throughout the ISO 9000 Standards, is "the output of a process." Such output is called "hardware" (physical items), "software" (information usually associated with computer systems), "processed materials" (materials from continuous processes), and "services" (usually delivered by a person). Often the output of an organization is a combination of these items.

4.0   Quality Systems Requirements

This section defines the features and characteristics of a quality system. Organizations are assessed against this section of the Standard. Some key terms used in the Standard are:

Supplier	=	the organization applying ISO 9001
Customer	=	its customer
Subcontractor	=	its supplier
Operator	=	anyone in the organization
Product	=	output broadly defined to include both goods and services
Shall	=	a requirement of the Standard that must be met
Notes	=	explanations which are not necessarily requirements

4.1   Management Responsibility

The management and control of quality within an organization must be the responsibility of its executive management.

Executive management must define a quality policy. This policy should address the activities of the organization and the needs and expectations of its customers. It must be communicated to and understood by employees at all levels of the organization. This policy must be the basis of a quality system, which will assure that the policy is implemented and maintained.

Executive management must define and document the responsibilities for implementing the quality policy and delegate the necessary authority. Management must provide the resources required for the implementation of the quality policy and ensure that assigned employees are adequately trained.

A Management Representative for Quality must be identified to take responsibility for the establishment, implementation, and maintenance of the quality system. This executive, at minimum, should provide management oversight of the system; associated tasks may be delegated. This person must also keep executive management informed of the operation and effectiveness of the quality system.

Management must review the progress of the organization against its defined objectives. The reviews must be formal, and records must be kept. The frequency of these reviews ensures that management controls and is aware of the performance of the quality system. Most organizations schedule Management Reviews every one to three months.

4.2   Quality System

This section establishes the need for a documented quality system. The system needs to include a quality manual and procedures. The quality manual relates the system to the ISO 9000 Standard by referencing the corresponding parts of the documented quality system to the ISO 9001 requirements. Procedures document the organization's processes.

Detailed work instructions for carrying out the organization's processes may be needed. The need and level of detail depend on the qualifications and experience of the personnel performing the tasks. Work instructions need to relate to the procedures.

A separate quality plan is not needed, provided the documented quality system defines how quality requirements are met. New projects, either initiated from within or required by a customer contract, need a quality plan if existing systems do not sufficiently define how quality is to be achieved. The quality plan requirement is a recognition that the quality system must change to ensure control as the organization develops. Such quality plans need to be integrated into the quality system.

4.3   Contract Review

Every order and contract with a customer must clearly define the goods or services to be provided. Prior to accepting a contract or order, the organization must verify its capability to complete the transaction. A contract exists when an offer by one party is unconditionally accepted by the other party. It need not be a written legal document. For example, a catalogue order constitutes a contract.

ISO 9000 requirements should be applied to all offers made by the company. The details of the offer need to be clearly articulated, and the organization must have the wherewithal and capability to provide what is being offered. When this is not possible, the terms and limitations of the offer need to be defined and included in the offer. For example, a seminar or concert provider offers seats, but only subject to availability.

The acceptance of an offer is normally in the form of an order. Orders may be written or verbal, depending on the nature of the business. Verbal orders need to be recorded. The details of an order should be reviewed to confirm that they are understood, are in accordance with the offer, and can be fulfilled.

The processing of contracts and orders, and possible changes to those contracts and orders, need to be defined. It is especially important that all those who need to know are made aware of the contract and order changes.

4.4   Design Control

In the design of a product or service, control procedures must ensure that all activities are performed and that records of work and results are generated and maintained throughout the design process.

Design needs to commence with a plan which defines milestones, responsibilities, and due dates; assigns qualified personnel; and provides necessary resources to the work. Design plans need to be reviewed and updated as the project progresses.

The relationships between the design function and other groups and functions, both inside and outside the organization, must be defined. A process must be established for efficient communication and interaction with other groups and functions.

The design process starts with inputs which are normally product requirements or product briefs. Relevant statutory and regulatory requirements relevant to the product must be included in the requirements.

The output of the design process is normally in the form of specifications and drawings which define the product or service. Critical features of the design must be identified and "acceptance criteria" established. The design is then evaluated to determine if these requirements are met. All output documents need to be reviewed and approved prior to the release of the product or service.

The design should be reviewed at defined stages by interested parties such as those in sales, purchasing, production, quality, and, if appropriate, the customer. Design verification can be achieved by calculation, comparison with proven designs, tests, or demonstrations.

Once the design meets requirements, it should be validated. Validation can be by prototype, model, initial production batch, or pilot delivery of a new service. During the validation, further tests are carried out.

Changes to the design need to be documented and approved before being implemented.

4.5   Document and Data Control

All documents relating to the quality system must be controlled, and procedures defining this control must be established. Document control means that changes to documents are only made by a proper authority, and only current/pertinent issues are available. Controlled documents include quality system documents (quality and procedure manuals and work instructions). Other controlled documents are product specifications and drawings, sales and product literature, and externally-produced documents such as standards and customer and supplier specifications.

The content of the organization-produced documents must be reviewed and approved by authorized personnel. This can be any member of the organization and can be the same person who prepared the document. The position needs to be defined in the document control procedure.

Changes to documents must be reviewed and approved by the function that initially approved them.

Changes made to documents must be indicated on those documents by an updated revision or issue level. A method for removing or marking all obsolete documents needs to be defined and a distribution list maintained.

Where data is on a computer system, there must be a procedure to ensure its security and safe storage. This requires a procedure for controlling the production and storage of backup data and the control of access to data through methods such as passwords.

4.6 Purchasing

Purchased products and services must meet the requirements for which they are intended. ISO 9000 has three requirements—the use of qualified suppliers, precise descriptions of what is purchased, and verification of incoming goods.

The Standard requires the evaluation of subcontractors whose products and services impact the quality of the products or service provided by the organization. Subcontractor or supplier evaluation can be done in a variety of ways, depending on how critical the purchased product or service is to the quality of the products and services of the organization. The evaluation may be based on a supplier's past performance or performance on trial orders. The supplier's quality system can also be evaluated either by third-party assessment, such as ISO 9000, or by second-party assessment. Whatever method is used, it must be defined and documented in a procedure.

For control purposes, purchase orders can specify that the products or services being purchased shall be supplied within a registered quality system such as ISO 9000 (although this is not a requirement of the Standard). If you require that your suppliers be registered, the order must fully define the title, number, and issue of the Standard, *e.g.*, ISO 9001: 1994 Quality System.

Purchasing documents need to clearly define the product or service being purchased either by detailed descriptions or by reference to catalog numbers, specifications, or other technical data.

Before orders or other purchasing agreements are released, they must be reviewed and approved by designated personnel. Verbal orders must be recorded and maintained, including reference to the subcontractor.

It is the responsibility of the purchaser to verify that purchased products and services are as ordered. Verification can be done visually or by inspecting/testing key product characteristics. ISO 9001 does not specify how an incoming product is verified. Each organization determines what is appropriate.

If verification on the supplier's premises is desired by either the organization or its customer, it must be specified in the purchase order. ISO 9000 does not require on-site verifications. On-site verification by the customer does not remove the organization's responsibility to ensure that the supplier performs.

4.7   Customer-Supplied Product.

In some business relationships, the customer supplies material, parts, documents, equipment, or tools to its suppliers. ISO 9000 refers to these items that are owned by the customer as customer- or purchaser-supplied material, or free issue material.

Some examples are parts sent to a subcontract plating firm for plating and special labels for placement on a customer's products. In service industries, customers may supply information and documents. Records should be kept of the receipt of such items, and the items should be kept in a safe place. Lost or damaged items need to be reported to the customer.

4.8   Product Identification and Traceability

Product identification is a means of positively identifying either in-process parts or completed items. Where identification is obvious, there is no need to introduce an identification system. For example, apples and potatoes can be identified by appearance, so there is no need to label them. If, however, different varieties of a product are stored together, it may be necessary to introduce a labeling system. Documents, which are usually the products of a service business, can be identified by title, number, date, and revision.

Traceability is a means to identify and locate products that have critical components or were produced from a particular batch of materials. In some industries where concerns of health, safety and environment are an issue, traceability is a requirement. In the pharmaceutical, food, and aerospace industries, traceability is common. Traceability can be requested by the customer or required by industry or government regulation.

Organizations may also implement traceability for their own purposes. If a product liability claim is filed, for example, traceability can help identify the date of purchase and the supplier of critical components. If a warranty claim arises, traceability can establish the date of production.

4.9   Process Control

Process Control requirements apply to all processes used in the production or supply of products and services. In manufacturing environments, these are typically inventory control, purchasing, fabrication and production, assembly, and test processes. In service environments all processes that contribute to the delivered service are included. For example, for a personnel agency seeking ISO 9000 registration, the process of selecting candidates comes under the requirements of this section. (In a manufacturing plant, personnel recruitment is outside the scope of the Standard.)

All processes necessary to produce, deliver, install, and service a product should be performed so that quality policy and objectives are achieved. Organizations must employ the necessary resources to ensure this. A means of control should ensure that what is required is actually done, and accompanying records kept.

Instructions such as procedures, specifications, recipes, drawings, etc. are needed "where the absence of such procedures can adversely affect quality." The complexity of the process and the qualifications of the employees doing the work determine whether or not instructions are necessary. (A thorough explanation is found in *Achieving ISO 9000 Registration*, by Owen, Cothran, and Malkovich, available from SPC Press, Knoxville, Tennessee.)

The Standard requires that equipment used in the operation of a process be suitable for the process. The quality of products and services must determine suitability of equipment. Procedures may be required to assess equipment suitability and provide maintenance to ensure continued process capability.

Where external standards, codes of practice, legislation, plans, or procedures are applicable, the quality system must determine and ensure that they are adhered to.

The standard of quality required is defined by specifications, tolerances, examples, illustrations, or similar means. These specifications should illustrate or define both what is acceptable and what is not. The standards can be specific to certain products or operations, or they may be generic to process outputs.

"Special processes" are those where it is not possible to determine from the output whether or not the processes have been successfully carried out. In these cases, verifying that the output is to specification can be accomplished by controlling and recording process input parameters, by testing (and thereby destroying) extra products or items, or by using qualified operators who can demonstrate their control of the process by special tests.

An example of a special process is precision welding. Weld penetration can only be confirmed by cutting the weld. A sample weld, with the same parameters as the required weld, can be tested to "qualify" the process and establish a level of confidence in the process. Other examples are heat treatment of steel, cooking of soufflés, etc.

4.10   Inspection and Testing

Process outputs (products and services) must conform to specified requirements. Verification can be done by any suitable means—even inspection by the process operator. ISO 9000 does not require independent inspections or any kinds of tests. The organization determines what is suitable to ensure quality. This section of the Standard addresses receiving, in-process, and final inspection and testing.

Not all purchased material needs to be inspected. Purchased items must be verified to confirm that they meet requirements. The method of verification is left to the organization. It needs to relate to the nature of the items, their source, and their importance to quality.

When purchased items come from an approved source and are clearly identified, verification can be based on physical observation and the supplier's documentation. In reality, customers accept the majority of items they purchase on this basis. Inspecting or testing purchased items is beyond most buyers' expertise and can be counterproductive.

When purchased items are tested or inspected, they should not be released until the results are known. If they must be released earlier, there should be a method of identification for possible recall.

In-process inspections and tests may be necessary to confirm that components, products, and services are to specification. These tests can be carried out by the process operators. Records indicating such verification must be kept. Where verification is required, the release of the items should be controlled until the verification results are known.

Prior to delivery to the customer or finished goods inventory, confirmation is required that all specified inspections and tests have been completed and there are no concerns outstanding. The authority for the release must be defined and a record kept of who authorized each release. The organization must define the mechanism for releasing products and services, and records should demonstrate that such policy is implemented and effective.

4.11 Control of Inspection, Measuring, and Test Equipment

When measuring devices and equipment are used to verify product or service quality, the instruments must be accurate and job-appropriate. Measuring equipment should have a known accuracy of at least 10% of the tolerance band of the measurement.

The accuracy of measuring equipment is determined by comparing its measuring performance to the performance of "masters" of known accuracy. This is the start of a chain of checks that needs to be traceable to national or physical standards. The link to national standards must be demonstrated by documentation.

The Standard requires a formal calibration program that includes all necessary information and instructions for calibrating equipment. Equipment should be labeled so that operators know the calibration period. Adjustable calibrated equipment must be sealed to prevent unauthorized adjustments. ISO 9000 auditors are interested in seeing calibration certificates from outside bodies.

Calibration must be done under special environmental conditions when needed for the accuracy of the measurements or to simulate where the measuring equipment is used.

4.12   Inspection and Test Status

When products and components are inspected, the outcome must be clearly indicated. This may be done on accompanying documents, by where the product is placed, or by marking the product.

This clause also applies to service organizations which require records for verification.

4.13   Control of Nonconforming Product

Items not conforming to their specifications have to be identified and/or segregated to prevent their use. A means of disposing of nonconforming items must be established and documented. There are four possibilities:

1. Items may be reprocessed or reworked to bring them back to specifications. The items would then meet the requirements after reprocessing and could be used.

2. The items may be accepted by a "concession." A concession gives permission to relax the specification for certain items or periods only. The design authority and/or the customer (if appropriate) must approve. The items may be used in the original non-conforming condition or reworked to a more acceptable level—but still not to specification. For example, a cabinet may be dented, but the dent is in the back and not visible. If the customer agrees to accept it anyway, this would be an example of original nonconforming condition. If the dent is on the front and clearly visible, the customer may agree to buy the cabinet, but only after the dent is filled and the cabinet repainted. The cabinet still may not be to specifica-

tion, but it would be acceptable. In either case, documented acceptance by the customer is required.

3. The items may be regraded and used for different applications. This can include blending faulty material with good.

4. The items may be scrapped and disposed of. The method of disposal needs to be defined to prevent re-use of the items.

4.14   Corrective and Preventive Action

The philosophy of ISO 9000 is to produce and provide goods and services that meet certain specifications, and when they don't, to make the necessary changes and improvements. The changes and improvements should not only be remedial to correct the problem (corrective action), but must also prevent the cause of the problem and its recurrence (preventive action).

Executive management must ensure that the corrective and preventive action process analyzes shortfalls in performance, identifies corrective and preventive actions, and ensures that such actions are effective.

4.15   Handling, Storage, Packaging, Preservation, and Delivery

The Standard requires the products, components, and materials to be preserved and protected in handling, storage, packaging, and delivery. These activities must be included in the documented quality system.

For controlled usage, dates must be tracked on items and materials with limited lives. Procedures need to be in place to control items requiring special storage conditions such as temperature, hygiene, and humidity levels.

The contract with the customer must specify the party responsible for delivery, and documentation must show that the products were delivered in accordance with the contract requirements.

4.16   Control of Quality Records

The operation of the quality system produces records which demonstrate the operation and effectiveness of the quality system. They must be readable and stored for a defined period in a manner that allows easy retrieval. The period is not specified in the Standard but should relate to the life of the product. If the product has only a short life, *e.g.*, fast food, there is no point in retaining records for years. If the product has a life of several years, records need to be kept for years. In some instances the contract specifies the length of time for record retention.

Hard copy, microfilm, and electronic media are all acceptable means of keeping records. If electronic media are used, precautions must be taken to ensure retrievability and readability, especially when computer hardware changes.

4.17   Internal Quality Audits

Required internal audits of the quality system are used to confirm that the quality system is being operated as defined. These audits must be planned and performed by employee auditors who are independent of the area being audited and who are trained in auditing techniques. The results must be recorded and reported to executive management.

When noncompliances are found, the responsibility for corrective action belongs to line management. The effectiveness of these actions is confirmed by subsequent audits.

Internal audits are not meant to confirm compliance to ISO 9000 requirements. Compliance must be built into the quality system when it is designed and documented.

4.18   Training

The qualifications for each position in the organization must be defined. Employee records should show current qualifications—

skills, experience, education, and training of employees. When assigning work, employee qualifications must match the requirements of the job.

4.19   Servicing

Where the contract specifies the servicing of a product, the servicing must be done within the quality system. The discussion in Section 4.9, Process Control, applies to this section.

4.20   Statistical Techniques

In practice, it is left to the organization to decide when and if it is appropriate to use statistical techniques for controlling processes and establishing product acceptance. When statistical techniques are required, they are part of the documented quality system and performed under controlled conditions. Employees using such techniques need to be trained and qualified.

Appendix C
Implementation Plan Guidelines

	Number of Months to Register		
Time Line for Activities: (See Chapter 6 for additional activity details)	8	12	18
Phase A - Analyze and Evaluate Existing Processes			
1. Prepare for the project • Training • Project plan	*1	1	1
2. Analyze and evaluate existing process	1	2	2-3
Phase B - Optimize and Document the Quality System			
3. Optimize the processes	2-4	2-6	3-10
4. Document and approve the quality system • Procedures • Work instructions • Quality manual • Procedure manual	2-4	2-6	3-10

* Table entries show calendar months in which activities are completed.

	Number of Months to Register		
Time Line for Activities: (See Chapter 6 for additional activity details)	8	12	18
Phase C - Implement, Operate, Refine the Quality System			
5. Train Internal Auditors and Prepare to Operate • Initiate the internal auditing program • Issue the documentation • Train the work force	5	7	11
6. Operate and refine the quality system	5-8	8-12	12-18
7. Verify readiness	7	10	15
Phase D - Registrar Audit and Registration			
8. Prepare for registration audit	7	11	17
9. Registrar audit and registration	8	12	18

* Table entries show calendar months in which activities are completed.

Appendix D
Lists of Procedures

Manufacturing Company – ISO 9001

Chap 8 Book (other)
Certif Book

1. Order Entry and Tracking
2. Inquiries and Proposals
3. Customer Returns and Complaints
4. Product Development
5. Supplier Approval
6. Purchasing and Receiving
7. Material and Inventory Control
8. Process Planning
9. Assembly
10. Packaging and Shipping
11. Product Service and Repair
12. Handling Nonconforming Materials and Products
13. Calibration
14. Maintenance of Equipment
15. Preventive and Corrective Action
16. Training
17. Control of Quality System Documentation
18. Control of Product Documentation
19. Management Review
20. Internal Audits
21. Control of Software Systems
22. Statistical Tools

Service (Trucking) Company – ISO 9002

1. Long Term Contracts
2. Customer Complaints
3. Inquiries and Quotes
4. Orders and Dispatch
5. Distribution and Delivery
6. Managing Customer Property
7. Equipment Maintenance
8. Calibration
9. Control of Data Processing Programs
10. Purchasing and Receiving
11. Job Requirements and Training
12. Control of Documentation
13. Management Review
14. Internal Audits
15. Corrective and Preventive Action

Appendix E
Sample Procedure

ACME Manufacturing	Proc. Number: 3
Jonathan Division	Effective Date: 10/31/93
	Revision: A
	Revision Date: 3/14/94
	Page 1 of 3

CUSTOMER RETURNS AND COMPLAINTS

Approved By:

Customer Service Manager   Date

General Manager   Date

Management Representative for Quality   Date

1.0   PURPOSE

To ensure that timely and appropriate remedial and corrective action is taken in response to customer returns and complaints.

2.0   SCOPE

2.1   Product returns, product complaints, and need for field repairs.

2.2   Any problem with any order.

This procedure is a controlled document and must not be copied in whole or in part.

ACME Manufacturing
Jonathan Division

CUSTOMER RETURNS AND COMPLAINTS

2.3   Any indication of dissatisfaction by a customer or prospect.

3.0   RESPONSIBILITIES

3.1   Customer Service administers the customer complaint/return system and maintains a file of all customer problems.

3.2   All employees receive complaints and report them to Customer Service.

4.0   PROCEDURE

4.1   Customer Service receives all complaints and indications of dissatisfaction and problems from the customer directly or through any employee. These are received, logged, and entered into the Customer Service system daily.

4.2   Customer Service prints the Customer Service Report (Appendix A) and assigns responsibility for follow-up. The responsible person acts to remedy the problem and takes action to correct and prevent recurrence of the same or similar problems.

4.3   If a remedy involves returned parts or products, Customer Service initiates a Return Authorization Form (Appendix B) for the customer. Returned materials are clearly identified on receipt and are processed per Procedure #12.

4.4   Customer Service monitors progress on complaints/returns and, after resolution, sends the customer a Problem Resolution Report (Appendix C).

4.5   Customer Service summarizes and analyzes all customer problem instances for the Management Review Meeting. Preventive and corrective actions that result are assigned, coordinated, and controlled through the Management Review, Procedure #20.

This procedure is a controlled document and must not be copied in whole or in part.

ACME Manufacturing
Jonathan Division

Proc. Number: 3
Effective Date: 10/31/93
Revision: A
Revision Date: 3/14/94
Page 3 of 3

CUSTOMER RETURNS AND COMPLAINTS

5.0   RELATED PROCEDURES

5.1	Management Review	Procedure #20
5.2	Handling Non-Conforming Materials and Products	Procedure #13
5.3	Repair	Procedure #12

6.0   DOCUMENTATION

6.1	Customer Service Report	Appendix A
6.2	Return Authorization Form	Appendix B
6.3	Problem Resolution Report	Appendix C

7.0   RECORDS

7.1   Forms and Problem Resolution Reports are filed in Customer Service by customer in date order and are retained for at least two years.

[Note: The appendices referred to in the procedure are not included.]

This procedure is a controlled document and must not be copied in whole or in part.

Appendix F
Changes in ISO 9000 Standards

The original ISO 9000 Standards were introduced in 1987 by the International Organization for Standardization. Their roots can be traced to the 1979 British Standard BS 5750 and the military Standards of NATO. A five-year review policy allows for the periodic review and amendment of the Standards. The 1994 version, on which this book is based, replaced the original 1987 Standards.

The next version of the ISO 9000 Standards is now being developed by an ISO 9000 committee. It originally was to be published in 1997, but that is not likely (the 1994 version was scheduled for 1992). While the changes in the 1994 version were not substantial, it is expected that the next revision will be more far-reaching. The next edition of the Standard will most probably be restructured and include requirements for staff recruitment, marketing activities, and additional features associated with total quality management.

It is too early to determine the extent of changes and additions already-registered organizations will have to make to comply with the late-1990s revision. How registration had been approached will certainly impact the magnitude of the effort to remain compliant. We are confident that if you achieve registration using the Process Management Approach, the magnitude of change and amount of work will be less for you than for those who used other approaches.

Appendix G
Where to Go for Help

The authors provide consultancy assistance, training materials, and training courses in North America and Europe. The rest of the world is covered by affiliates. For further information, you may call or write to the authors or the following organizations.

The authors' earlier book, *Achieving ISO 9000 Registration: A Process Management Approach to the Optimum Quality System*, provides a detailed description of how to gain registration. It is a book, written by practitioners for the staff who need to become practitioners, and it addresses in detail all the issues associated with achieving registration. The book may be ordered directly from the publisher whose address is on the following page.

In Europe

Dr. Bryn Owen
Optimum Systems for Quality, Ltd.
Simonstone Business Park
Simonstone, Lancs. BB12 7NJ – U.K.
Phone: 01282 779002
Fax: 01282 779099

In North America

Peter M. Malkovich
East Concord Associates
5512 Concord Avenue
Edina, Minnesota 55424
Phone: 612-927-0860
Fax: 612-927-5313

In North America

Process Management International
7801 East Bush Lake Road,
Suite 360
Minneapolis, Minnesota 55439
Phone: 800-258-0313
Fax: 612-893-0502

To Obtain Copies of the ISO 9000 Standards:

In the United States	ASQC Customer Service Department P.O. Box 3066 Milwaukee, WI 53201-3066 Phone: 800-248-1946 Fax: 414-272-1734
In Canada	Standards Council of Canada (SCC) 45 O'Connor Street, Suite 1200 Ottawa, Ontario K1P 6N7 Phone: 613-238-3222 Fax: 613-995-4564
In the United Kingdom	British Standards Institute 389 Chiswick High Road London W4 4AL UK Phone: 0181-996-9000 Fax: 0181-966-7400
Rest of the World	Contact your National Standards Organization

To Order Additional copies of this book or the book—*Achieving ISO Registration: A Process Management Approach to the Optimum Quality System*—please contact:

SPC Press, Inc.
5908 Toole Drive, Suite C
Knoxville, TN 37919 U.S.A.
Toll free Order Line: (800) 545-8602
Phone: (615) 584-5005
Fax: (615) 588-9440